T. 76.

Sciurus Volans   Guajacana

Flying Squirrels
GLIDERS IN THE DARK

A SMITHSONIAN NATURE BOOK

Nancy Wells-Gosling

Smithsonian Institution Press
1985

To David

Frontispiece: The first illustrations of the North American flying squirrels were provided by Mark Catesby.

Photographic credits

All photographs are by Nancy Wells-Gosling except where otherwise noted. The species of flying squirrel is identified either within the caption or by an abbreviation immediately following it.

Jim W. Grace, whose photographs also appear in this book, is with the U.S. Forest Service.

Library of Congress Cataloging in Publication Data

Wells-Gosling, Nancy, 1953–
    Flying squirrels.

    (A Smithsonian nature book)
    Bibliography: p.
    Includes index.
    Supt. of Docs. no.: SI 1.2:S95
    1. Flying squirrels. I. Title. II. Series.
QL737.R68W33   1985   599.32′32   84-600310
ISBN 0-87474-952-2
ISBN 0-87474-951-4 (pbk.)

Contents

Foreword

Flying squirrels have a way of becoming part of people's lives. The first flying squirrel I met revealed itself late one autumn afternoon, when a heavy curtain exhibited a sinuous motion from floor to window top. The pilferer of nuts from the bowl on the living room table, and cacher of nuts under couch and chair cushions, was discovered. That squirrel went to school with me. Later there was Skitter, a northern flying squirrel of enormous personality. Even Skitter's beginning was out of the ordinary; he had been captured as an infant by a Siamese cat in Mariposa, California. Skitter starred in numerous television programs with Dr. Robert T. Orr of the California Academy of Sciences before he moved east with me.

Dr. Robert S. Hoffmann at the University of Kansas put Nancy Wells-Gosling in touch with me in 1980. Since then we have shared our admiration for flying squirrels through letters and in the squirrel sessions we enjoy annually during meetings of the American Society of Mammalogists.

Flying squirrels are a necessary part of Nancy Wells-Gosling's life. She admitted her addiction in her first letter:

I keep caged colonies of both species . . . as well as one of each as house pets. They are fascinating creatures and we become very attached to them—not the ideal situation for an aspiring researcher, I suppose.

I would argue that it *is* the ideal situation. So would the ethologist Hans Kruuk, who usually has either a hyena or a badger at home. Dr. Kruuk makes his case:

There is no better way to get the "feel" of the behavior of an animal than to have one constantly around the house.

In June 1981, after attending the mammal meetings in Oxford, Ohio, I drove north with Nancy to visit the Goslings' *Glaucomys* sanctuary in southern Michigan. We arrived late at night. David Gosling greeted us at the door, closely followed by three inquisitive, in-house flying squirrels.

Although the A-frame house was built by David, an entomologist, he must have had flying squirrels in mind. Up the long draperies they climb to sail across to a beam. From there, after head-bobbing to gauge distances, they launch to glide and land across the room on stair rail or sofa back. Impeccable housekeeping prevails at the Goslings. The only visible concession to the presence of the small goblins is a dish of applesauce, with powdered Esbilac mixed in, on the coffee table, and a few hickory nuts stashed among cushions.

The guest room, in the apex of one end of the house, was part of the home range of one squirrel. From balcony rail to door top he scampered, then to the ceiling beam, along the beam to the door top and out again. I timed his circuits and soon fell asleep.

Next morning, when the flying squirrels were denned, I met their daytime replacement, Havoc the red squirrel. He had spent the night inside a hard hat on a high shelf. It was evident that Nancy's interests included *all* North American tree squirrels.

Outside in the woodland clearing are the compounds, one for southern flying squirrels and one for the northern species. Den boxes and tree limbs make the walk-in enclosures miniature habitats.

Nancy and David have become so squirrel-like in their habits that they pick up bushels of hickory nuts each autumn, hulling and hoarding them for their flying squirrels.

At the mammal meetings, where Nancy and I swap squirrel stories, T-shirts are almost a uniform, worn by distinguished professors, museum curators, and graduate students alike. Nancy saw the potential market and soon produced T-shirts, in several sizes and colors, with a flying squirrel in full glide and block-lettered legend "Fly Glaucomys."

The late William P. Harris, an authority on squirrels, often wrote to me about the Huron Mountain region of Michigan's Upper Peninsula, a place he loved above all others. He was president of the Huron Mountain Wildlife Foundation, which supports research projects on the 17,000 acres of virgin hardwood and coniferous forest composing the Huron Mountain Club. It would have pleased Mr. Harris to have a flying squirrel researcher at Huron Mountain, and to hear her pronounce the area "undoubtedly the nicest wilderness in Michigan." He would have smiled at the unexpected problems that Nancy, like all field biologists, faced, from a trap-happy pine marten to the gadabout mother flying squirrel that left her with six newborn babies.

Nancy Wells-Gosling pays tribute to her companions in research in this addition to the Smithsonian Nature Book series. Her long hours of careful observation, her empathy with squirrels she came to recognize, and her detailed photographic records reveal much about the lives of these small squirrels that are so much a part of her life.

Dorcas MacClintock
Curatorial Affiliate, Peabody Museum
of Natural History, Yale University

Preface

Sometimes a small object can change one's life dramatically. In my case, it was a two-ounce bundle packaged in gray fur, complete with two enormous, dark eyes. I had often dealt with orphaned wildlife but this foundling struck an especially responsive chord; I determined at once to learn everything possible about flying squirrels.

Many years later, I still have not accomplished that goal and, of course, I never shall. Nevertheless, the endeavor has been thoroughly enjoyable. I have had the pleasure of getting to know many fascinating flying squirrels as well as scores of wonderful "squirrel persons."

For their part, the squirrels have vividly demonstrated to me what being a flying squirrel is all about. The humans have generously, and often humorously, shared their accumulated knowledge of flying squirrels. Because one person can gather only so much firsthand information in a lifetime, such communication is invaluable, especially when dealing with animals so difficult to observe under natural conditions. I am grateful to all those people who freely shared their flying squirrel lore with me, especially A. L. Albers, J. B. Jarboe, B. J. and M. Gagler, J. A. King, W. Lawrence, M. Majneri, M. C. Nielsen, A. K. Petruska, P. R. and C. S. Reedy, L. Silvermann, N. Sloan, and F. Stehr.

Much of what I have written in this book was gleaned from other authors, and I have tried to credit the source of my material in the text. Readers can then check the bibliography to be guided back to the original publication, if they so desire. The literature is rich, varied, and fascinating to read, but to a large extent anecdotal. Plenty of opportunity remains for further flying squirrel research. I salute all those who have made the effort in the past and wish to thank the following for providing me with much valuable data and helpful advice: A. C. Avenoso, J. E. Crider, P. J. DeCoursey, D. S. Hall, J. G. Hall, D. W. and A. V. Linzey, R. A. Mowrey, I. Muul, F. L. Pogge, R. A. Shook, T. Shook, D. F. Sonenshine, R. C. Stojeba, and P. D. Weigl. My investigations of flying squirrels in the Huron Mountains of Michigan's Upper Peninsula were supported by the Huron Mountain Wildlife Foundation.

I am indebted to the following people for assitance in reviewing my manuscript: S. Anderson, R. Block, I. J. Cantrall, D. E. Corsi, P. J. DeCoursey, J. R. Giacalone-Madden, D. C. L. Gosling, E. Gould, D. S. Hall, L. R. Heaney, K. E. S. Kirby, B. S. Low, R. A. Mowrey, K. K. Petruska, E. F. Rivinus, R. W. Thorington, and P. D. Weigl.

I also thank Dorcas MacClintock, author of *Squirrels of North America*, for writing the foreword to this book.

Southern flying squirrels have been the focus of most of my squirrel-watching and this is quite evident in my writing. People chiefly familiar with northern flying squirrels may have to make an allowance for my bias as they read the book. I have tried to state clearly whenever I was specifically referring to northern flying squirrels; otherwise I probably had southern flying squirrels on my mind as I wrote. It is not that I prefer the southern species to their boreal relatives. Quite simply, my southern flying squirrel subjects and I are kindred spirits, raised in the oak-hickory woodlots of southwestern Michigan. I know them better.

1. *We Are Introduced*

On a chilly May morning in 1976 my husband, David, stepped outside to fill the bird feeder, as was his usual custom. This time, however, he returned almost immediately. Extending his arm toward me, he opened his gloved hand to reveal a tiny, furred animal. With its large eyes, loose skin, velvety gray-brown fur, and flattened tail, what else could it be but a young flying squirrel?

I reached down to touch the squirrel and he instantly grasped my finger with his forepaws, setting teeth against my skin. He did not bite but seemed to be warning that he could defend himself if necessary. Gently I inspected the delicate creature. The fur on his back was fine and softly textured, with a subtle intermixing of gray and gray-buff hairs. As I stroked against the lay of the hair, the charcoal-gray underfur was prominently exposed. In striking contrast, the fur on his underside was a clean cream-white.

The squirrel was singularly handsome. Enormous, dark eyes were his most appealing feature, endowing him with a gentle, intelligent expression rarely possessed by rodents. His large, nearly naked ears perked forward inquisitively, and long black whiskers shimmered around his muzzle. Only partially grown, perhaps five weeks old, he measured 18 centimeters (7 inches) from the tip of his nose to the end of his tail. His tail was already developing the flattened, featherlike appearance typical of flying squirrels.

A loose fold of skin extended from the wrist of the forearm to the ankle of the hindleg along both sides of his body. At its outer edge, where top and bottom met, the fur was distinctly darker. Pulling gently, I could draw out the flap several centimeters. This flap, called the patagium, is a feature unique among North American mammals. When mature, the squirrel would be capable of long, graceful glides through the nighttime forest by extending his legs and stretching the patagium as an airfoil.

At such a young age, the squirrel was still dependent upon its mother and could not have survived on his own in the wild. He had probably tumbled to the ground during the night, unhurt, while exploring near the entrance to his family's nest. Had David not seen him cowering in the flowerbox under our window, a prowling dog or cat surely would have. I mixed a milk formula and offered an eye-dropperful to the frightened animal; the sustenance was eagerly accepted.

Like most people I had rarely encountered flying squirrels. They easily escape notice, being the only nocturnal squirrels in North America. In southern Michigan, where I live, the numerous diurnal relatives of flying squirrels are well known and widely recognized. These include fox squirrels, gray squirrels, and red squirrels, as well as chipmunks, woodchucks, and ground squirrels. Seeing a flying squirrel is a rare treat, even though they are often as abundant as their sun-loving counterparts.

In fact, flying squirrels frequently nest in attics or roofs of houses, remaining undetected by the homeowners unless they become too noisy while chasing each other or rolling nuts about at night. In other cases, their presence is revealed when their high-pitched chirps and squeaks distress the sensitive ears of the family dog. We guessed our young waif had lived with its family under our roof. The discovery of a small perforation in the eaves and half-eaten hickory nuts on the ground below confirmed our suspicions.

Infrequently seen, flying squirrels are often deemed rare animals, restricted to small, select areas. Quite the contrary is true. Two species reside in North America and together cover a broad portion of the continent, their ranges overlapping slightly. Fortunately for me, both species occur in Michigan with their ranges meeting in the northern portion of the state. Thus, as my interest in flying squirrels grew, I was able to study them conveniently in their native habitats. Superficially the two species look very much alike, and I first had to acquire proficiency in distinguishing between them at a glance, because under field conditions a glance may be all one gets of a fleeing squirrel. Initially this seems difficult, even with a specimen in hand. A few key characters must be carefully evaluated. Eventually, with experience, identification occurs almost by gestalt; one forms a general image not only of the physical qualities, but also the distinctive character and behavior of each species.

A five-week-old southern flying squirrel is a mere handful.

The southern flying squirrel, *Glaucomys volans,* is the smaller of the two, measuring 20–25 centimeters (8–10 inches) in total length and weighing 60–120 grams (2–4 ounces). As its name implies, this species ranges farther south than the northern flying squirrel. Its fur is not thick. Individual hairs of the pelt are 10–12 millimeters (about ½ inch) in length, lying down neatly to give the animal a sleek, lustrous appearance. For most of its length the hair is charcoal-gray, but the last two millimeters are light gray tinged with brown. Unless the fur is parted or shows wear, the charcoal gray portion is hidden and the tip of the hair gives the squirrel its characteristic coloration. This may range from almost steel-gray in some individuals to a rich gray-brown in others.

A southern flying squirrel's breast is cream-white and when the fur along its midline is parted, one can see that these hairs are white their entire length. This is an important feature for distinguishing between the southern and northern species. Although northern flying squirrels also have light-colored undersides, the hairs are a sooty color and are often tipped with shades of gray or brown. The hairs have lead-gray bases, which can be seen when the fur is parted.

To avoid confusion, only hairs along the squirrel's midline should be examined for this characteristic. On some southern flying squirrels, hairs near the legs have light gray bases which can mislead one to suspect the animal is some type of hybrid. In addition, older southern flying squirrels often display colorful tinges of orange-brown on the hair tips along the flanks or under the patagium.

Northern flying squirrels, *Glaucomys sabrinus,* are larger than their southern relatives. In total length they measure 25–37 centimeters (10–15 inches) and weigh 110–230 grams (4–8 ounces). Adults vary in color from light tan to rust-brown. The finely textured hairs are 16 millimeters (⅝ inch) or more in length, and do not lie down as neatly as those of the southern flying squirrel. These two factors make the pelage thicker and more insulating. As a result, the northern flying squirrel's appearance is somewhat hirsute and robust, the facial profile in particular being more rounded than that of the southern species.

Even a very young flying squirrel sports long, full whiskers, called vibrissae. (SFS)

The gliding skin, or patagium, extends from the front to the hind legs along both sides of the squirrel. (SFS)

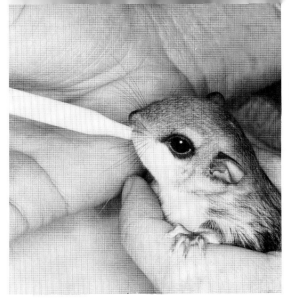

An orphaned southern flying squirrel dines on milk from an eyedropper.

Newborn of both species have naked, ratlike tails, but within two weeks, fine fur appears, and in three weeks the lateral hairs elongate, producing the flattened, featherlike appearance. In adults, the tail composes 40 percent of the total length of the animal. Southern flying squirrel tails are 16 millimeters (5/8 inch) thick from top to bottom, with the underside distinctly white. Northern flying squirrel tails are dense and feltlike, being as much as 20–30 millimeters thick (up to 1¼ inches). They are more uniformly colored and are only slightly lighter on the underside. A dark tail tip is a common feature in northern flying squirrels.

In both species, juvenile flying squirrels can be distinguished from adults in several ways. Besides being smaller, they are drab gray, with only faint traces of brown. Their fur does not completely acquire distinctive adult coloration until they complete their first molt at between three and six months of age.

If one is not careful, the juvenile pelage can lead to confusion in identifying the animals, as I once learned to my chagrin. While studying flying squirrels in the Huron Mountains of Michigan's Upper Peninsula, near Lake Superior, I lived in a forest abundant with northern flying squirrels. At least four families regularly visited a feeder outside my door and at times it seemed like a three-ring circus, with as many as a dozen squirrels crowded onto the feeders at once. Although the adults were a bit wary, the juveniles promptly accepted my presence. The porch light illuminated their feeding site and I spent many enjoyable hours on my back doorstep watching them.

One evening, two new and rather skittish juvenile squirrels arrived at the feeder. Smaller than the other juveniles, they were, I assumed, much younger, perhaps venturing from the nest for the first time. Extremely tense, they ran away at the slightest disturbance.

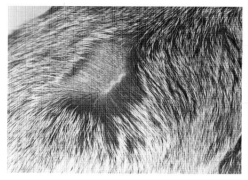

When the fur on a southern flying squirrel's back is parted, the hairs are seen to be gray-brown at the tips, but charcoal-gray for most of their length.

To my astonishment, the following evening an adult southern flying squirrel appeared at the feeder. I recognized her immediately by her distinctively white underside and nervous disposition. Only then did I realize that the shy, flighty youngsters were also southern flying squirrels, her offspring. Their drab juvenile pelage was not sufficiently distinctive for me to immediately recognize their species identity in a location where I was not expecting them.

The discovery of these animals provided an important new locality record because they were 65 kilometers (40 miles) north of the known range for southern flying squirrels in that part of Michigan. However, I could have missed this important record entirely if the distinctive adult squirrel had not arrived to jar me to my senses. Suddenly, with hardly any effort on my part, I had the perfect opportunity to compare the behavior and watch the interactions of the two flying squirrel species.

Soon it became apparent that the northern flying squirrels arrived at the feeder first each evening, gliding in from points 10–30 meters (33–100 feet) away. From left and right they swooped in long, graceful arcs that ended with an abrupt upturn, allowing each to land safely on the hard tree trunk.

After one squirrel landed, it turned and hung on the trunk, alertly surveying the situation with limpid, dark eyes. Satisfied all was safe, it climbed down to the feeder. A sudden movement nearby sent it scampering back up the trunk, but it returned a few moments later if no threat materialized. Presently, as many as six or eight squirrels quietly shared the feeder, crowded side by side, while others foraged on the ground below or climbed through nearby trees.

Their manner was calm and deliberate. The young were especially casual and fearless; I was able to walk up and gently scratch their backs or stroke their heads as they fed. Adults were not quite so trusting. I was allowed within a meter of where they sat, but could not touch them. When I tried, they bounded up the trunk and waited for me to retreat.

Twenty minutes after the northern flying squirrels started to feed, the southern flying squirrels arrived in a flurry. I never discerned the exact direction from which they came; they simply appeared on a

The adult southern flying squirrel (left) is distinguished by its bright, cream-white underside. The adult northern flying squirrel, (right) has a sooty white underside.

nearby tree. With a short glide-jump they cleared the gap to the feeder tree. I usually glimpsed the bright flash of white belly fur as an adult made this leap, but failing that clue, I could instantly distinguish a southern flying squirrel by its behavior at the feeder tree. Nervous and flighty it made several fast feints down the trunk toward the feeder, but quickly retreated, sometimes emitting a strident "chittering" call. Reassured that the surroundings were safe, it rushed back to the feeder at which several northern flying squirrels were already feeding. The explosive arrival of their smaller relative sent them flying in all directions. Any northern flying squirrel bold enough to remain on the feeder was summarily driven off. Most retreated without resistance and did not fight for a place on the platform.

Once at the food, the southern flying squirrel was more alert and fidgety than the northern flying squirrels. With quick, birdlike movements it picked up sunflower seeds, shelling them to eat. Disturbance nearby put the animal instantly on the alert, sending it shooting to the back of the trunk or up it out of sight.

Cautiously, the northern flying squirrels reapproached the feeder. Again they were rebuffed. But eventually, one of them refused to be harassed further and unhurriedly pulled itself onto the feeder. As if recognizing its bluff had been called, the southern flying squirrel sat at the opposite end of the board and continued to eat, suspiciously eyeing its larger relative. The other northern flying squirrels adjusted to the situation by waiting for their southern cousin to leave or by picking up seeds beneath the feeder. They foraged about on the ground or went crashing loudly through the nearby underbrush.

I was indeed fortunate to have the opportunity to watch both species at one feeder; similar situations have been reported only a few times before. For the most part, the squirrels occupy exclusive ranges and in regions where their distributions overlap, habitat preference supposedly keeps them separate. When one encounters a flying squirrel in the wild, identifying the species to which it belongs often is possible simply by noting its geographic location or habitat. However, I suspect that where range overlap occurs, they share local habitats more commonly than is generally supposed. Both squirrel species are very adaptable.

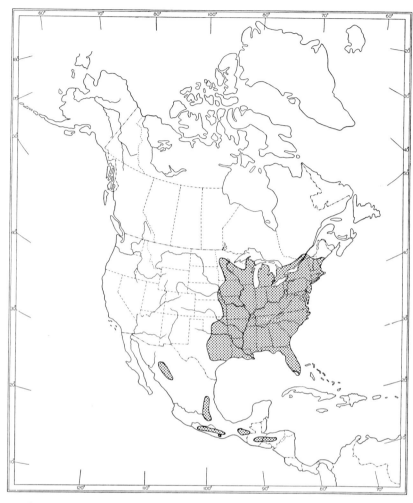

North American distribution of the southern flying squirrel.

Southern flying squirrels have often been referred to as eastern flying squirrels because the major portion of their range corresponds closely with the boundaries of the eastern United States. Four subspecies occupy the United States and Canada; a subspecies being a geographically distinct population that can be distinguished from another subspecies by some physical trait, such as size or color. The northernmost locality record is in southern Quebec at a latitude of 45°30′ N, that is, about as far north as Montreal and Ottawa. The western boundary of their range is defined by the treeless Great Plains; after all, a flying squirrel needs launching sites.

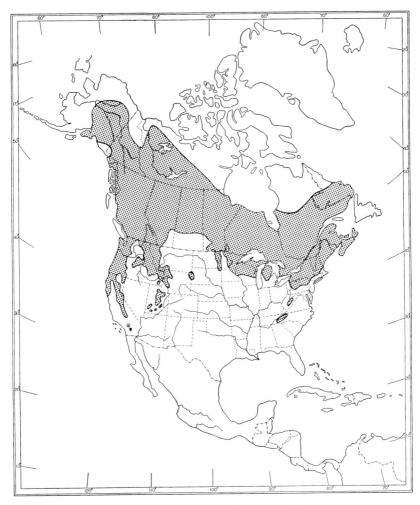

North American distribution of the northern flying squirrel.

Four isolated subspecies of southern flying squirrels have been found in Mexico and Central America where they inhabit mountainous, dry oak-pine habitats and cloud forests. Some biologists have suggested they form a third species of flying squirrels. Unfortunately our knowledge of their life history and biology is negligible. This does mean, however, that the opportunity exists for a young field biologist to make his or her professional reputation studying these animals to fill in the gaps in our knowledge. When we know how southern flying squirrels live and behave in middle American climates and habitats we will know much more about the genetic flexibility of the species and the effect of environment on life history strategies.

In the United States, southern flying squirrels are found in a variety of forest habitats, ranging from the dry brush country of eastern Texas to the mixed conifer-hardwood forests of the north to the extensive pinelands of the southeast. I consider oak-hickory woodlots the best habitat for southern flying squirrels in southern Michigan because a variety of food, especially nuts, is produced. Beech-maple forests have been cited as another favored flying squirrel habitat in our area, but I have not found the squirrels abundant in such forests. These tree species allow the production of many nesting sites because they readily form cavities, but food production is often neither reliable nor sufficient.

For example, in 1981 I located six groups of southern flying squirrels in the Huron Mountains, all inhabiting mature maple forests with numerous cavities and a few scattered oak trees. Local residents informed me the previous autumn had been one of abundant acorn production. After a poor acorn year I suspect I would have a difficult time finding squirrels in the same location, or anywhere in the region for that matter.

The twenty-five subspecies of northern flying squirrels cover an extensive continental range from the Pacific to the Atlantic coasts. Northernmost records come from the cold boreal spruce forests of central Alaska and the mouth of the MacKenzie River in the Northwest Territory of Canada. From there the squirrels range across Canada to Labrador.

In the eastern United States, the southern border of their range is in the northern tier of states, although isolated populations are irregularly distributed at elevations of 1200 meters (3,900 feet) or more in the Appalachian Mountains as far south as Tennessee and North Carolina. These montane squirrels are probably relicts from the early postglacial age 10,000 to 15,000 years ago when temperatures were much cooler. Currently, they seem to be declining in numbers, and North Carolina lists the northern flying squirrel as an endangered species.

On the Pacific coast the northern flying squirrels range from Alaska southward along the coastal mountain range to northern California, and in the Sierra Nevada their range extends southward into California. The Rocky Mountains harbor gliders down to southern Utah and eastward through Wyoming to the Black Hills of South Dakota.

Covering such a wide span of latitudes and altitudes, the squirrels also occupy diverse habitat types. Appendix A lists some of the forest types in which flying squirrels have been found. Their adaptability is quite remarkable.

2. *Gliding in the Dark*

To me, the flying squirrels' New Year begins in late February when winter thaws come. More snow will certainly fall again before winter relinquishes its grip, but for awhile, at least, the ground may be almost bare. Sap begins to flow in some trees, and at the far end of our woodlot, small wounds oozing sweet fluid appear in the bark of a large, imposing maple. Southern flying squirrels are once again actively foraging after long weeks of quietude; they eagerly seek the sweet sap by gnawing away bits of tree bark.

Dressed warmly against the evening cold, I place a handful of seeds and cracked nuts at the base of the maple and wait for dusk to fade. The temperature may vary between $-7°C$ and $+7°C$ $(20°–45°F)$ but I know this will have little effect on the time of the squirrels' arrival. Only if the mercury drops below $-10°C$ $(14°F)$ might they fail to appear. Likewise, wind has little influence unless it is a very strong breeze that wildly thrashes the trees and makes gliding a bit too exciting and hazardous. A moderate wind merely makes the squirrels nervous; they have difficulty discerning which noises proclaim danger and which do not. If it rains, I leave their evening meal, but don't bother to wait. They will come to the feeder, but at an unpredictable time, and each squirrel will stay only a few minutes.

Light level is the best indication of when the squirrels will arrive at my feeder. While studying the internal clocks, or circadian rhythms, of southern flying squirrels, Patricia DeCoursey of the University of South Carolina showed that the animals become active in the evening when light decreases to an intensity between 1 and 6.5 foot-candles. The average was 3.4 foot-candles, a level that occurs about thirty minutes after sunset. This varies because, like humans, each squirrel has its individual schedule. Some are early birds, others are late risers.

Of course, human eyes do not measure light level in foot-candles, but my rule of thumb is to occasionally glance at the maple tree 2 meters (6 feet) away. When details of the tree's bark can no longer be discerned in the failing light, I know a squirrel will arrive imminently.

With luck, I'll catch sight of a squirrel 20 meters (63 feet) away and can watch as it glides unerringly toward the maple tree where I wait. The small form slices through the air beneath the tree canopy, veering left or right to avoid tree trunks and branches. It might easily be mistaken for a floating leaf except that on such a calm evening

19

no leaf could be driven so far through the woods.

Two meters from the maple tree the glider makes a sudden, sharp upward turn. Its white underside flashes in the dim light as its body swings into a vertical position, bringing all four feet to the front for landing. In an instant it contacts the trunk, the only sound being that of tiny claws digging into bark.

Without any delay, the squirrel dashes up the tree trunk or sidles around back out of sight. This evasive action probably helps foil any pursuing predator, such as an owl. The landing and subsequent dash for safety blend into one continuous motion. Where one stops and the other starts is difficult to say. Then, for a long moment, the woods once again seem devoid of flying squirrels. Satisfied it is not being chased, the squirrel finally comes around the trunk to survey the night's ration.

Almost invariably, the first arrival is an adult female, the "boss" of the feeding station. Being accustomed to my presence, she glances at me only momentarily before running headfirst down the trunk to the base of the tree. Cracked hickory nuts are the choicest food items and she selects these first. Climbing back up the tree with the fragment in her mouth, she settles on a branch stub to eat. She balances on her hind feet with her back toward the trunk, and arches her tail over her body in a graceful, sigmoidal curve.

By this time another squirrel, either a mature male or subadult, glides in and warily climbs head first down the tree trunk. Should the first squirrel still be occupied with her food, the second arrival can snatch a portion of nut and move up the opposite side of the trunk. However, if the female has consumed her morsel and is ready for more, she chases the intruder away. Spiraling the trunk, they scurry in the rapid, sidling motion typical of flying squirrels, chattering angrily. Finally, the harassed newcomer leaps to a tree several meters away and runs up out of harm's way, to return in a few minutes once the dominant squirrel is again preoccupied with a nut.

I may see as many as four squirrels and am kept entertained by the flurry of activity for about twenty minutes. Then the squirrels' immediate hunger pangs are allayed and things calm down a bit. If pieces of hickory nuts remain, they continue to remove them, storing the food for later use. Aided by my headlamp, I can watch as one of the squirrels climbs far up into the tree branches to wedge a piece of nut into a convenient crotch, pounding the food firmly into place with its front incisors. Seated on the ground 15 meters (50 feet) below, I can clearly hear the vigorous, rapping noise.

To speed its return to the ground for more nut fragments, the squirrel leaps off the tree and spreads its patagium to pancake down in a smooth, cork-screwing glide, landing on the trunk only a meter above the food.

When all hickory nuts are removed, the squirrels start consuming sunflower seeds. These smaller items are not worth carrying off one at a time or fighting over, so one or two squirrels sit on the ground with their backs to the tree, shelling and eating seeds. Some squirrels prefer to feed while hanging by their hindfeet over the pile of seeds, occasionally reaching down to rake up another tidbit. Thirty or forty minutes after their arrival the squirrels are satiated, for the time being, and activity decreases even though some seeds remain. Over ensuing hours squirrels will occasionally return for a snack, but dinner is over. It is time for me to retire.

Two to six squirrels visit my feeder in February. By June, after the spring litters begin foraging, I can count as many as eight. While studying the mixed group of southern and northern flying squirrels in the Upper Peninsula, I counted at least twenty-eight squirrels visiting the feeder outside my door. At the peak of their activity there were squirrels everywhere, on the feeder, scaling tree branches, hopping in the underbrush, running on the porch railing, even hanging from the rafters.

To the best of my knowledge, however, no one has reported seeing as many flying squirrels foraging in one location as John James Audubon and the Reverend John Bachman claimed to have observed. In 1851, they wrote:

We recollect a locality not many miles from Philadelphia, where, in order to study the habits of [flying squirrels], we occasionally strayed into a meadow containing here and there immense oak and beech trees. . . . Suddenly . . . one emerged from its hole and ran up to the top of a tree; another soon followed, and ere long dozens came forth, and commenced their graceful flights from some upper branch to a lower bough. At times one would be seen darting from the topmost branches of a tall oak, and with wide-extended membranes and outspread tail gliding diagonally through the air, till it reached the foot of a tree about fifty yards off, when at the moment we expected to see it strike the earth, it suddenly turned upward and alighted on the body of the tree. It would then run to the top and once more precipitate itself from the upper branches, and sail back again to the tree it had just left. Crowds of these little creatures joined in these sportive gambols; there could not have been less than two hundred. Scores of them would leave each tree at the same moment, and cross each other, gliding like spirits through the air, seeming to have no other object in view than to indulge a playful propensity. We watched and mused till the last shadows of day had disappeared, and darkness admonished us to leave the little triflers to their nocturnal enjoyments.

So many flying squirrels congregated within viewing distance is hard to imagine. How would one keep track? The closest record to this I could uncover occurred in Lebanon, Pennsylvania, where in 1949 a homeowner supplied peanuts to the flying squirrels living in his wooded tract. Eventually he claimed to have seen as many as 100 animals sailing around among his trees. Southeastern Pennsylvania must be prime flying squirrel territory.

Computing reliable population density figures for flying squirrels is difficult. A habitat may provide excellent conditions one year, unfavorable conditions the next, depending on food production. In winter, the squirrels often nest in groups, resulting in overestimation of their abundance if a survey is conducted near a concentration. Shy and trap-wary in early summer, the squirrels can give the impression of being absent or rare in a woodlot where they are actually quite common. Recruitment into a population occurs as juveniles disperse, so densities in southern Michigan are at their highest in early autumn after two summer breeding periods are completed. They gradually decline until early spring when the new litters are born.

By late February, the 2-hectare (5-acre) woodlot near my home supports about six squirrels, the lowest it will be all year. Therefore, the return of flying squirrels to the feeding station in February is not merely a reminder that winter cannot persist for many more weeks. It also heralds the renewal of life. The southern flying squirrel mating season is underway, ensuring the arrival of young by April.

Flying squirrels usually manage to keep their nocturnal courtship modestly hidden from human view. Our knowledge of its details is fragmentary and comes from watching captive squirrels, obtaining occasional glimpses of activity in the nighttime forest, and extrapolating from our understanding of other squirrel species. Southern flying squirrels have been studied more than their northern relatives, so describing their family life is easier. However, my experience with both species suggests that such a description also provides a reasonable portrayal of events in a northern flying squirrel family, at least in Michigan.

To fully understand what happens in February, one must turn back to late summer of the previous year. By July's end the mating season is concluded and male squirrels lose their ability to impregnate females. Their testes gradually decrease in size and retract into the abdominal cavity. Males in this condition are appropriately referred to as "abdominal" and have no sexual interest in females throughout the autumn and early winter.

While a graduate student at The University of Michigan, biologist Illar Muul studied the effects of day length on male southern flying squirrels and concluded that their sexual metamorphosis is controlled by changing photoperiod. In Michigan, squirrel testes start shrinking after the summer solstice; the passing of the year's longest days being the important signal. Not all male squirrels undergo the transformation at the same time or rate, but once it starts it is a rapid change, usually completed in less than three weeks.

A distinct change in male squirrel temperament also occurs at this time. They go from being aggressive and nervous to timid and somewhat complacent. I find it suddenly becomes much easier to handle captive males with less danger of being bitten.

From August through November, male southern flying squirrels remain abdominal. As the winter solstice approaches, their testes begin to enlarge. Again, the time and rate of development varies among individuals. Changing light conditions provide the signal, but an animal's response is affected by many factors, such as age, weather, nutrition, and general health. Young males born in late summer may or may not mature sexually in time for the spring breeding season. However, by mid-January all adult males are scrotal.

Even then, they still might not produce viable sperm for several more weeks, and mating definitely does not occur until the females are prepared. Noticeable external signs of their sexual receptiveness do not appear until at least mid-February.

During the weeks prior to mating, squirrels in my woodlot and captive colony share their winter nests, aggregating for communal warmth. However, upon first showing signs of estrus, a female becomes the object of intense interest to the males. Domestic tranquillity is disrupted. Squabbling and agitated scolding can be heard anytime, day or night, and sometimes the squirrels erupt from the nest in the middle of the day.

Detailed accounts describing flying squirrel courtship and mating under natural conditions are lacking. Occasionally a pair is seen momentarily, sometimes even in broad daylight, but most activity occurs after dark or within the safety of the nest or other shelter.

Diurnal squirrels have been studied in much more detail because of the relative ease of making direct observations. As increasing numbers of observations on squirrel mating behavior become available, certain distinct, though not inflexible, patterns become evident. Quite likely, flying squirrel nuptials will be found to fit one of these patterns so it is worthwhile to look at the general trends. Recently they were summarized by Lawrence Heaney of The University of Michigan Museum of Zoology.

As Heaney stated, squirrels have "mating bouts" in which groups of males, up to a dozen, gather near a female during the one day she is receptive, although they may start visiting her home range a few days previously. The males attend her closely. Many people are familiar with the rather comical "trains" of fox or gray squirrels, loping through the trees or across the ground in single file. The female leads; the males follow. However, in squirrels of the genus *Tamiasciurus*, which includes the red squirrel and Douglas squirrel, the males apparently cannot tolerate being so close to each other. They are dispersed throughout the female's home range, though remain intent on keeping track of her location.

In either case, certain males tend to be dominant. These remain closest to the female and usually do the actual mating because they are able to repel other males. Dominant male Douglas squirrels are often those with home ranges adjacent to the female's, whereas dominant gray squirrels are usually older animals with high standing in the squirrel social order. In most species, however, females have been observed to solicit copulation with subordinate males either after mating with the dominant male or by somehow evading his companionship.

Presumably the dominant male is the "best" animal, being strong or aggressive enough to repel the others. He should be the sire of choice for the female's offspring, passing on the genes that enabled him to become top dog in squirrel society. Why, then, should a female accept, and even solicit, subordinate males? No one knows for certain, but that doesn't stop biologists from speculating.

For instance, in some species matings with several males can result in the young of a single litter having different fathers. In that case there would be wider genetic variation among a female's offspring, an advantage when environmental conditions are uncertain. Matings with subordinate males might help reduce inbreeding. Young tree squirrels tend to establish home ranges near their mothers. A dominant male living close to a female might be that female's own offspring or other close relative. A mating between the two would result in inbreeding, which has been shown to be harmful to many wildlife species. A subordinate male that has come from some distance is probably not closely related.

There are other, tentative explanations why a female might accept several males, but whatever the true reason or reasons, it is profitable for a male to do considerable traveling in search of an estrous female. If he mates, his genes will be passed on to the next generation. The females will not come to him, so nothing is gained by staying home. While conducting a radiotelemetry study of red squirrels I monitored a male that covered as many as 500 meters (1,650 feet) in a single direction in one day searching for a female. The next day he would be 500 meters in another direction. I suspect he was occasionally successful in perpetuating his genetic constitution even though his wanderings eventually cost him his life (and cost me a radio collar which he took with him to an unknown grave).

Where do flying squirrels fit into this scheme? How many squirrels engage in the mating bouts? We don't know. No one, to my knowledge, has reported seeing more than a pair of squirrels courting in the wild. However, in my colony of caged squirrels, an estrous female usually accumulates a retinue of males during her receptiveness. The squirrels squabble all day, and, occasionally, the female will break out of one nestbox and escape to another, with a male in hot pursuit. By evening four or five males may be vying for her with vigorous chasing around the cage. By the time mating occurs, usually about nine or ten o'clock at night, one male has managed to repel all the others and he copulates with the female. Occasionally another male will attempt to interrupt the pair, but rarely is he successful.

Will the female mate with more than one male, or a subordinate male, as tree squirrels do? Again, we don't know. Immediately after mating a large, mucilaginous plug sometimes blocks the female's vagina, a condition that occurs in many female rodents. This mass is exuded by the male and probably functions to keep other males from copulating with her until she is fertilized. Thus, successive matings might not be productive.

How far do males travel to court a female? Which males, if any, tend to be dominant? Sadly, these questions have not yet been answered.

If my caged southern flying squirrels are any indication, the mating season is short and frenetic. Within ten to fourteen days all the mature females have experienced estrus and have probably mated. Thereafter, the squirrels lapse into sleepy lassitude to wait out the final weeks of winter.

However, as the forty-day gestation progresses, a female becomes increasingly intolerant of her nestmates. A week or two before giving birth, she seeks out a retreat of her own. It may be a hollow tree, an abandoned woodpecker excavation, a fox squirrel's previous leaf nest, or any suitable crevice or nook. Her search is intense and may lead her to investigate bird houses, garage corners, attics, and even chimneys.

Once a location is chosen, the female furnishes it with the most suitable materials available. I have found nests made of shreds of bark from juniper, grapevine, or other plants. However, pieces of soft cloth, paper, string, moss, grass, hair, rabbit fur, shredded leaves, wool, or feathers make fine additions to the nursery furnishings.

The expectant mother becomes exceedingly secretive about her new home; if an intruder comes near she sits quietly in a hidden vantage point as long as necessary, waiting for it to depart. That is, unless the intruder is another southern flying squirrel.

No other flying squirrel is tolerated near the primary nest site and under certain circumstances this protectiveness expands to include the entire home range. Biologist Jacalyn Madden, while a graduate student at City University of New York, found females maintaining

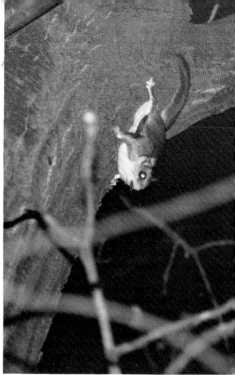

Pregnant females have ravenous appetites. (sfs)

Hind feet like grappling hooks let a flying squirrel defy gravity and feed from a safe height. (sfs)

exclusive home ranges, defended against both sexes. Trespassers were unceremoniously confronted and driven away; the matron stamping her feet and lunging, launching a physical attack if necessary to convey her message. Madden hypothesized that all the resources necessary to raise a family were evenly distributed throughout the study site. By establishing an exclusive claim over a portion of habitat a female had access to all the requisites for successfully rearing a litter of young. Interlopers would siphon off some of those vital resources and were not allowed to remain.

Antagonism at feeding stations is most evident during this period of the year. An adult female "owns" the feeder and all others take second place. They must sneak in and grab seeds or nuts while the dominant female is occupied with her meal, or wait until she is satiated. The female will not even suffer the male that sired her offspring. He cannot assist in raising or protecting the babies and has no further role in their upbringing.

Meanwhile, the nesting aggregations of males and nonreproductive females begin to dissolve at about the same time as do the winter snows. Although pairs and small groups of animals continue to share nests throughout the summer, these assemblages are decidedly amor-

A female southern flying squirrel peers from the entrance to her nursery nest.

phous. Each squirrel moves independently, sometimes sharing a nest for a night, sometimes living alone.

Courtship and mating behavior of northern flying squirrels in the wild is even more of a mystery than that of southern flying squirrels. However, comparing those I have in captivity with their southern kin, it appears their reproductive patterns are similar. For instance, males undergo the distinct seasonal changes in reproductive condition on about the same timetable. Female northern flying squirrels enter estrus much later than southern flying squirrel females, usually not until mid- to late March. But that is to be expected in Michigan's Upper Peninsula where winters are long and severe. In addition, only one litter is produced per year, so maternal duties do not have to be rushed.

Clearly, flying squirrel reproductive behavior is a big unknown. When we finally learn more about it, will the pattern be similar to that of diurnal squirrel species? It remains a fruitful field of study for an intrepid researcher, with superhuman night vision.

3. *Bringing Up Baby*

Early April seems a harsh time to bring tiny, helpless squirrel pups into the world. Southern Michigan's bleak transition from winter to spring can be accompanied by cold rains or several inches of burdensome snow. Sharp winds whip the tree tops with frightening force. On the other hand, promising intervals of warm sunshine brighten the days and during the long, mild nights woodcocks twitter their courtship rites in the lowland field beyond my woods.

The southern flying squirrel mating season is short and the spring season of birth is similarly abbreviated. Almost all the litters are born within the first two weeks of April, unless winter was unusually harsh. When courtship and mating are delayed by the weather, the spring litters also will be tardy by several weeks, of course. It always seems to me that once the schedule has been disrupted, the relative synchrony of births also disappears and litters are born over a wider time span.

The female makes final preparations for her confinement by restlessly gathering whatever soft fibers are available. Meticulously she lines the nest interior with material she has reduced to fine shreds by holding it in her forepaws and tearing it with her incisors. By this method even coarse bark becomes a soft, pliable bed. As her time draws near, she retires within her nest, not to reappear until twenty-four hours or more after she has given birth.

Observing squirrels in captivity, I find the female's behavior an unmistakable portent of birth. White "froth" protrudes from the nestbox entrance hole as the cotton I provided for nesting material is thoroughly fluffed up. On seeing this, I move the nestbox to a private compartment.

For two or three weeks following birth, the female leaves the nest for only brief respites from her maternal duties. Having selected and furnished a well-protected, snug nursery, she ensures that her family can endure inclement spring weather in relative comfort. Later, when the young are making heavy demands upon her and then learning to forage on their own, the fullness of late spring and then summer will fulfill their needs.

Only once have I glimpsed the birth of a flying squirrel. Glancing inside a nestbox to check on a captive female, I found her in the midst of parturition. I did not linger for fear of distressing her further, so I could only observe that she was sitting back on her haunches with body hunched over, presumably to assist with the process. On the bedding before her lay one tiny, pink baby curled on its side. When I investigated a few days later, she was brooding three healthy infants.

Litter size varies. Sometimes only one pup is delivered. In my experience this is particularly true for young females giving birth for the first time. Subsequent litters are usually larger.

Then there is the other extreme. I once captured a very large, pregnant northern flying squirrel in jack pine habitat in the Upper Peninsula. David facetiously noted her remarkable resemblance to a sack of watermelons. A few days later she gave birth to six pups. This was an unusually large litter, as I was soon to become acutely aware. Given a chance to escape several weeks later, the female did so most ungallantly, leaving me to nurse her abundant family on an eyedropper. Their manners were atrocious and I got far more milk on them than inside them. It was a great relief when they finally began eating solid food at five weeks of age.

Average litter size for both species of flying squirrels is three, but two or four pups is not at all out of the ordinary. Large families of five or more can be a liability to a female. They make enormous energy demands upon her and unless food is plentiful, they all suffer.

For several days after giving birth, the mother squirrel hardly leaves the nest; even food is of little interest. She crouches over the young squirrels hour after hour, patagium spread like a blanket to keep them warm. Finally, when evening descends, she prepares to leave the nest for a short time. Carefully, she envelops the babies in soft

To form a nursery, this female northern flying squirrel has filled her nestbox to overflowing with white polyester stuffing.

Inside the nest the female broods her young by spreading her patagium like a blanket. (SFS)

nest material. Their tiny bodies lack a covering of fur and they need to be well insulated.

Before cautiously slipping from the nest she watches and listens several minutes for danger. Once outside, the female stamps and slaps her hindfeet vigorously to start circulation flowing again; after many hours in a confined position her muscles are cramped and stiff and suppleness must be coaxed back into them.

This accomplished, she devotes a few minutes to some much-needed grooming. She draws her forepaws together over her face, starting behind the ears and progressing to the nose, repeating the process several times in rapid succession. The session ends with a quick combing of the tail. Twisting sideways she grasps and draws it with a rubbing motion between her forefeet from base to tip. Now she is ready to set off.

After a long winter, food is not always easy to find. Mild nights entice a few fluttering moths which the female pounces upon. She may find insects or spiders still confined to their winter retreats. A bountiful nut crop the previous autumn means good fortune; the highly nutritious nuts are still available in hidden caches. A dried piece of fungus, lichens, bark, or green tree buds may contribute to her meal. If hunger is severe and food scarce, some females will not pass up an opportunity to kill and eat a roosting bird.

She will not remain absent longer than necessary although her time out is well deserved. Having tended to her immediate needs, she returns to her family. In the morning, just before sunrise, she may again slip out for a few minutes.

The young are helpless should danger threaten while they are alone inside the nest, but if the mother is present she jumps to their defense with lightning-fast reflexes. She will box with her forefeet to discourage entrance to the nest and will sink her teeth deeply into an intruder if it persists. Inside a secure tree cavity with only one small entrance she can usually repel potential predators in this manner. Should one of her young be pulled from the nest, the female makes a lunging grasp, using teeth and forefeet to retain possession of her offspring. The unfortunate baby may be seriously injured if its mother is too forceful a defender.

Nevertheless, the week after birth can be an uncertain time for the pups; some mothers will readily abandon them under stressful circumstances. If a predator threatens and she can escape, the mother might desert, saving herself. This may seem cruel, yet if she abandons her family in a dangerous situation, she at least remains alive and can produce another litter later. If she lost her life, nothing would be gained; too young to fend for themselves, the pups would soon die as well.

Maternal steadfastness varies widely. It always seems to me that young females tend to be more fickle, experienced mothers more reliable; but this is not invariably true. Each individual is different. However, after a week to ten days have passed, a mother squirrel will usually take considerable risks to ensure the welfare of her babies, regardless of her earlier attitude. Her investment as a parent is, at that stage, quite large. Starting over again would require much energy and many risks, and the season is well advanced.

To be safe, I take special care with captive animals in the early stages of motherhood. Having their babies handled by humans can so upset some females that they will kill the young. I do not assume the maternal instinct will be strongly evident until the young are at least one week old. After that, the mother usually becomes a devoted parent, sometimes to the detriment of her own safety.

Many tales have been told describing the attachment of mother flying squirrels to their young. Perhaps the earliest account of this devotion was written by Audubon and Bachman:

> A piece of partially cleared wood having been set on fire, the labourers saw the flying-squirrel start from a hollow stump with a young one in her mouth; and watched the place where she deposited it, in another stump at a little distance. The mother returned to her nest and took away another and another in succession, until all were removed; when the woodcutters went to the abode now occupied by the affectionate animal, and caught her, already singed by the fire, and her five young unscathed.

J. W. Stack wrote in the 1926 *Journal of Mammalogy* of the "courage" shown by a flying squirrel mother. Forestry students were trimming trees when one sawed off a limb containing a flying squirrel nest with young. The mother escaped and the student carried the nest to the ground. As the group inspected the babies, the female glided from across the nearby river, landing at their feet. Scaling the pants leg of the student holding the nest, she grasped a baby, descended to the ground, climbed a nearby tree, and sailed back across the river to deposit her offspring in a new tree cavity. The performance was repeated four times. All the babies were retrieved directly out of the student's hands.

At other times a female will take great pains to move her babies to a new site when the nest becomes unsuitable for occupation, for instance, when the flea population becomes unbearable. She is familiar with all the available secondary nests within her home range and will carry the young, one at a time, to a new home.

A female accomplishes this feat by first nosing the baby onto its back. Using forefeet and mouth she juggles it into position and gently grasps it in her teeth across its stomach. Instinctively curling into a

A half-grown juvenile makes quite a load, but mother manages. (SFS)

ball when lifted, the youngster appears wrapped around the lower half of its mother's neck, "like a huge goiter," as it was once described. The female's movements are not hindered with the baby in this position.

The maneuver does not always progress smoothly. When in a hurry, the female may grab any convenient part of the baby, usually a leg or the patagium, but sometimes an ear or tail. The baby curls up as usual, but dangles awkwardly beneath the female. She then must stop and position the infant properly if she has far to go.

A female will not hesitate to glide while carrying a baby. Although her first effort might fall short if she fails to compensate for the additional weight, subsequent glides are right on the mark. Her head is held well back when climbing a tree trunk to prevent harshly rubbing the young squirrel against the bark.

Rescue missions occur even when the young pups have become quite large. Half-grown juvenile squirrels make quite a mouthful, but the female manages to transport them. When they gain some physical coordination at about three weeks of age, they assist by clasping their legs around her neck. Even the finality of death might not discourage her; one female pathetically retrieved babies that had been killed by a cat.

I have captured females needed for my studies by baiting them into live-traps using their own offspring as enticement. However, this ploy is not always successful. I once found a nest containing a mother and her week-old babies. The female immediately bolted for safety into a nearby tree cavity, leaving her offspring behind. Removing them from the nest I placed the young squirrels in a trap and quietly sat back to wait for their mother to rescue them. Once or twice the female peered out of her hiding place, but then disappeared inside and was seen no more. Even my efforts to imitate the distress squeaks of young squirrels were of no interest to her. Once again I found myself in possession of a family of young squirrels with no mother. Fortunately, a lactating female captive in my study colony served as wet nurse.

The mere sight of a displaced pup is one inducement to retrieve; sound generated by the baby is another. When distressed, a young squirrel emits high-pitched, rasping squeaks. At times the noise is beyond the limits of human hearing, but the forced heaving of the young squirrel's body reveals that it is calling.

Rather feeble at first, the vocalization gains volume as the squirrel grows, reaching full strength in three weeks. After that, increasingly rougher handling is required to make the youngster squeak, but it does so vigorously when necessary. After eyes open, at approximately twenty-eight days of age, the tendency to squeak gradually disappears. This varies from individual to individual, but juvenile vocalizations rapidly become more adultlike.

A human imitating these infantile squeaks can ignite a female into a frenzy of searching. If the sound is made through pursed lips, she may climb onto one's face, trying to locate its source. In one case, a southern flying squirrel mother insistently tried to rescue my index finger as I softly squeaked through my teeth. She refused to release me for a long time but eventually decided I was too large to carry off and tuck into her nest. After being deceived several times in this manner, most females learn to discriminate between a real distress call and human deception.

Illar Muul demonstrated the strength of the retrieving response in lactating females. He repeatedly presented young squirrels to a lactating mother and she dutifully carried them off one after another until she had retrieved fifty babies. The experiment was terminated at this point, not because the female showed signs of flagging, but because she was hyperventilating from her efforts and needed to rest. Babies rescued by a female do not have to be flying squirrels; she will also accept baby mice, rats, ground squirrels, and probably other rodents as well.

However, about forty days after giving birth, the females in Muul's experiments began attacking young squirrels from other litters. They would accept only their own babies and even these were rejected if they had an unfamiliar odor.

What might happen in the wild should a lactating female enter the nest of another mother while the latter was absent? Would the intruder kidnap very young babies, carrying them back to her own nest? I had

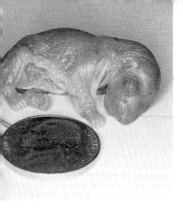

Newborn   One week old   Two weeks old

The growth of a southern flying squirrel.

to wonder about this once when I found two southern flying squirrel nests in the woods only 15 meters (50 feet) apart. One contained five young; the other harbored a single baby, and all were approximately the same age.

With the excellent care provided by their mother, young flying squirrels grow rapidly. Physical changes are noticeable almost daily. The following short description of southern flying squirrel development is a summary of my own observations and information from a paper published in 1979 by Donald and Alicia Linzey of Virginia Polytechnic Institute and State University. The Linzeys monitored a group of squirrels from birth to one year of age. I have found this information very useful for determining the age of litters of young squirrels found in the wild. Then by backdating I can determine their approximate time of birth, give or take a few days.

At Birth. The young squirrel is naked, except for a few short whiskers; its flesh is bright pink, with blood vessels and internal organs visible through the thin, delicate skin. Already the gliding skin is evident. Weight is 3–6 grams (0.1–0.2 ounces); total length is about 60 millimeters (2½ inches).

Eyelids are sealed shut but the eyes can be seen as dark orbs under the skin. Ear canals are also sealed, with the ear flap folded over on itself. Tiny claws are present although the toes are fused together. Sex of the pup can be readily distinguished.

Completely helpless, the pup usually cannot right itself when placed on its back although it flails about with forefeet. High-pitched distress squeaks are uttered to summon the mother. The infant is also capable of weakly clinging to objects with its forefeet. The main activities for the next several weeks are nursing and sleeping.

One Week. Darkening of the skin occurs on head and back while short hairs appear on the head, chest, shoulders, and along the mid-

Three weeks old   Four weeks old

line of the back. The animal's underside remains naked and pink. Ears now stand erect but the ear canal remains sealed as do the eyelids. The toes begin to separate and facial whiskers are 3–5 millimeters (⅛ to ¼ inch) long.

Some babies are able to right themselves at this age, but most struggle helplessly when placed on their backs. If the nest is disturbed they freeze and remain motionless. When lifted, they curl up as if being carried by their mother.

Two Weeks. The soft, downy hair covering the squirrel's face and back begins to acquire a brown tone while the chin and chest develop a fine covering of white fur. However, the abdomen and undersides of the chest and patagium remain naked. All toes are separated and the ear canals begin to open although the squirrel shows no indication of being able to hear. Facial whiskers are about 10 millimeters (⅜ inch) long. Within a few days lower incisors erupt. Weight is 10–15 grams (0.35–0.5 ounces) and overall length is about 105 millimeters (4 inches).

If placed on a flat surface the infant pushes itself backward. Placed on its back, it is able to right itself immediately, even on a smooth surface. Inside the nest the pup digs into the nesting material using its forelegs. Soon it is able to move its tail and facial whiskers voluntarily.

Three Weeks. The animal's coat is distinctly darker than before. Lateral hairs begin to develop on the tail and these soon give it a flattened appearance; already it is dark on top and light beneath. The eyelids are darkening and becoming better defined; soon they will gradually separate and the eyes will open. Hairs appear on the underside of the patagium, legs, and lower abdomen, but the skin is still visible.

The baby responds to loud noises and reacts with a jerk when touched. It seems to orient to familiar smells. If placed on a table the pup propels itself backward vigorously, all the while giving a loud rasping squeak. Tenaciously it clings with the forefeet to any nearby object.

Four Weeks. Measuring 150 millimeters (6 inches) in total length, the young squirrel weighs about 25 grams (0.87 ounces). Lower incisors are about 8 millimeters (5/16 inch) long and the upper incisors now erupt. Fur completely covers the body; the whiskers are 25 millimeters (1 inch) long; and the flattened tail is 8 millimeters (5/16 inch) wide. Eyes open.

At this point, a nest filled with three or four babies becomes a crowded and busy place. Although they do not yet leave the nest, the juveniles become increasingly active. Moving about energetically they sample bits of food the mother brings for herself. However, weaning will not occur for three or four more weeks. When handled, the young squirrels remain relatively motionless, not attempting to escape, and usually do not cry. They instinctively extend their legs to spread the patagium when they fall, but cannot yet glide.

Five Weeks. At this age a young squirrel weighs 30 grams (1.05 ounces) and has a total length of about 175 millimeters (7 inches). It has full juvenile coloration and is becoming increasingly active. If disturbed in the nest, the pup might display the defensive behavior of rolling onto its back and boxing with the forefeet, mouth agape, although it usually will not bite. Should the intruder be undeterred, the young squirrel then attempts to hide by pushing and crawling underneath objects or its littermates. When handled, it struggles mightily to escape and bites in self-defense.

Some exploration outside the nest is attempted, but the slightest disturbance sends all the juveniles scurrying back inside. Scuffling and arguing can be heard inside the nest as the playful young squirrels wrestle with each other, their mother, or their own tails. At times I have seen the mother abandon the nest, curling up outside to sleep, apparently to escape her rambunctious offspring.

Less information is available on the growth of northern flying squirrel babies. However, I kept records of seven families, born of adults captured in Michigan's Upper Peninsula and, in general, their rate of maturation roughly paralleled that of southern flying squirrels except that they were proportionally larger.

At birth, northern flying squirrels weigh 4–6 grams (0.14–0.20 ounces) and are about 70 millimeters (2¾ inches) in total length. During the ensuing weeks their fur develops in the same sequence as that of southern flying squirrels. When 20 days old, they first react

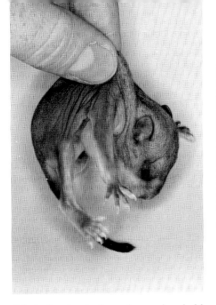

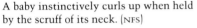

A baby instinctively curls up when held by the scruff of its neck. (NFS)

The orphaned mouse (right) was raised by a southern flying squirrel foster mother along with her own litter.

to sound, and their eyes open at 28 to 32 days. Lower incisors erupt at 18 days and the upper ones at 30 to 32 days.

For the initial four weeks of life, they, too, squeak in a raspy manner when distressed. Dutifully, mother rescues them, although it never seems to me that the northern flying squirrel female undertakes the task with the same urgency as does her southern counterpart. I have also noticed that a V-shaped layer of fat is evident under the skin of a pup's abdomen for the first ten days of its life, something I have never noticed in southern flying squirrel young.

By five weeks of age young northern flying squirrels weigh about 30 grams (1.05 ounces) and are approximately 175 millimeters (7 inches) in total length. Their fur is longer and softer than that of southern flying squirrels, and the feltlike tail is about 15 millimeters (½ inch) wide, but not distinctly bicolored.

From this age forward, squirrels of both species rapidly become more mobile and independent. This is an important period of their lives; they must learn how to survive in the dangerous, complex world outside the nest.

4. *Now Welcome, Summer*

As Michigan's cool spring days lead into summer, the daily routine of a female southern flying squirrel with growing family entails long hours of domestic duties interspersed with short foraging trips. Gradually the forays become more protracted as her hungry brood makes increasing demands. Fortunately, the pups are rapidly gaining strength. Longer periods on their own do them no harm.

Food is becoming more readily available and diverse. As an added benefit, the new covering of leaves on the trees helps hide her from hungry predators. This is a dangerous period for a lactating female. She must forage intently to keep pace with her family's needs at the same time that predator parents are facing similar pressures. Flying squirrels make a welcome meal, and caution is the order of the day.

In the woods, the secretive females do nothing to draw attention to themselves. Would-be observers find this a frustrating period for flying-squirrel watching. Even well-supplied feeding stations may be abandoned when the bounty of late spring, and then summer, provides a variety of fresh foods. Many times I have sat expectantly at my feeder tree to see only the flit of a tail as a squirrel passed, intent on finding a meal away from my prying eyes.

Males are as inconspicuous as the females. The initial mating season is concluded, and the next mating bouts are still many weeks away. There is no need to roam far and food is easily obtained.

Observing adults during the lactation period might be difficult, but seeing inside a woodland nest is next to impossible. As a result, family life, before the young commence exploring outside, is very much a mystery to biologists.

To pry inside this hidden world, I constructed a wooden nestbox equipped with a glass viewing window. Carpet lined its interior; no additional nesting material was provided, because I quickly discovered the female would use it to block the window for privacy. This nestbox was attached inside a cage, adjacent to a darkened blind. Using a dim red light for illumination, I watched through the window as a family of southern flying squirrels grew up inside their home. I spent an hour or two inside the blind every day, at different times of the day, to cover their entire schedule.

As might be expected, the first four weeks of infant squirrel life are rather monotonous to watch. Sleeping and eating are their nearly exclusive activities. Trying to keep from dozing off was mine. All the while, mother broods them, patagium spread like a warm blanket. With head tucked down close to the nest floor and front feet partially supporting her weight, the female almost totally hides her young. From this posture she can adjust the bedding with her forepaws, or scratch an ear with a hindfoot, without disturbing the babies.

Initially, the pups are barely noticeable under her, but as they grow, their oversized feet begin to protrude at all angles. Mother soon resembles a disorganized, mammalian caterpillar. On their backs, sides, or stomachs, with legs outstretched, the babies sleep, looking relaxed and comfortable indeed. When the female leaves the nest, all doze in a confusing heap of intertwined legs, tails, bodies, and heads.

The cramped quarters can become unpleasantly hot as days grow warmer and the babies, larger. After three weeks of crouching over her offspring, the mother switches to other, more comfortable positions. On her side she can cradle the young within her patagium. Lying on her back with legs and patagium outstretched to cool off, she holds the pups on top of her. Although rather ungainly looking, the position is undoubtedly more relaxing for her than spending long hours hunched over the babies.

As the young squirrels' eyes open and gradually come into use, the pups weakly pull themselves up to the nest portal to peer out when mother departs in the evening. However, it will be another week before the boldest of them crawls out to sit on the nestbox.

Safely sequestered for a few more days, the young squirrels rapidly become increasingly coordinated and vigorous. Between the ages of four and five weeks, many new behavior patterns emerge. Attempts are made to wash the face with forepaws, or scratch the head with a hindfoot. Nesting material is feebly pulled and rearranged. Although

As the babies grow, mother's patagium can no longer neatly envelope them. (SFS)

39

far from being weaned, the young squirrels begin to take an interest in solid food. Mother no sooner returns from a foraging trip than they sniff and investigate her mouth. Food is indelicately wrenched from her grip, whereas odd fragments of nut shells serve as playthings. The babies gnaw industriously with their short incisors.

When the squirrels reached this stage of development my observation periods became much more interesting and rewarding. I was taken by one remarkable similarity between young flying squirrels and human children; neither can keep their sticky fingers off clean glass. My vigil was regularly interrupted by the need to clean off the viewing window. The squirrels reacted to this by curling up and hiding in the nesting material. A few minutes after I finished, activity resumed.

Growing stronger each day, they play and wrestle; sometimes one bites too hard. A squawk of outrage brings play to an abrupt halt, but it soon starts again, as rough as ever. Farther and farther they hang out the entrance hole until at five weeks of age they can no longer be confined by the nest. One evening a juvenile follows its mother to sit outside. Almost as quickly, it retreats, but for the next several evenings the young squirrels experiment with short forays, never going more than a few hops from home.

The rambunctious pups are not inhibited by broad daylight. Like many other youngsters, juvenile flying squirrels have difficulty remaining still for long periods of time. Adults patiently sleep through the day waiting for darkness to descend before venturing forth, but naïve young squirrels are not as cautious. About midday, jostling and fighting can be heard inside the box as the infants frolic, and sometimes their exuberance cannot be contained. Suddenly, they will erupt from the nest and, seemingly unconcerned, chase each other about, always remaining close to safety.

However, most exploring occurs after sunset. With the young now leaving the nest, a patient and quiet human observer knowing the woodland address of a native flying squirrel family can spend many enjoyable evenings watching the squirrels. They readily tolerate illumination from a dim flashlight, and do not allow it to hinder their activity, although the light may make their mother rather nervous.

Shortly after dark the young squirrels tumble out of the nest directly behind their mother. No matter how eager they may be to follow and stay close to her, they lack sufficient strength and agility to keep pace as she forages. Therefore, with a strong, thrusting leap she leaves her bewildered offspring far behind on the nest tree.

Temporarily abandoned, the juveniles develop their stamina and coordination by climbing about in nearby branches. Fortunately, even as they become more intrepid and venture farther away, the

As they grow older, juveniles explore farther from the nest, thoroughly investigating each new object. (NFS) *Photograph by Jim W. Grace.*

mother retains her solicitous attitude. As Illar Muul and John Alley wrote in *Natural History:*

> . . . they begin short exploratory trips in the vicinity of the nest although any disturbance causes them to scurry quickly back to it. Sometimes, if a young squirrel's feeble limbs are not quite steady enough to support it on its elevated perch, the result is an inadvertent trip to the ground. A few cheeps, however, will bring the mother to the rescue.

Intently investigating the new sights, sounds, smells, and tastes of the world outside their nest, the juveniles nibble at tree buds and bark, fungi, or occasional insects, such as moths or May beetles. Flying squirrels relish insect fare but an inexperienced youngster finds an invertebrate's wildly flailing legs, equipped with spines and claws, a ticklish and formidable barrier. Vigorous, sputtering face-washing is the only remedy, and many an arthropod walks away unharmed until the young squirrel learns to deal with them. The capture of a wasp may have a less pleasant ending, but no permanent harm is done.

At six weeks of age weaning has begun and will be completed in a few weeks, although this varies according to the mother's attitude and the persistence of the young squirrels. They attempt to nurse as long as possible, but a conflict develops between parent and offspring. As zoologist Robert Trivers postulated, the two generations of animals, mother and young, face conflicting interests. For the mother, there comes a point when it is more advantageous to leave her family and start a new one, thereby increasing the number of offspring she produces in her lifetime. Her current pups, old enough to soon fend for themselves, make enormous demands upon her as long as they continue to nurse. This reduces her ability to reproduce again that year. Therefore, she must encourage their independence.

It is to the offspring's advantage, however, to receive care and nourishment from their mother as long as it even marginally enhances their ability to survive, grow up, and reproduce themselves. Hence, they attempt to continue nursing. There comes a time, though, when they receive almost no benefit from the relationship and could actually harm their own genetic fitness by reducing the number of half-siblings their mother would otherwise produce.

Trivers elegantly expressed his hypothesis mathematically, but for a field observer the conflict becomes apparent when the mother squirrel decides enough is enough. Outside the nest she will lie down and embrace the branch beneath her, denying the young access to her teats when they try to nurse. At other times, she simply shoves them away with her forepaws. They eventually get the message. I suspect some females resolve the conflict more emphatically. At least once I have found a nest of juveniles still bunking together, while the mother had moved to another nestbox on the other side of the woods.

Before young squirrels can become entirely independent, they must learn to get around in the world. Short jumps are attempted at first and these gradually lengthen into glides. Sometimes the mother encourages the initial efforts by calling from a nearby branch, as if urging her offspring to clear a small gap. However, flying squirrels don't need much coaxing. To them, gliding is as natural as walking. Soon they fearlessly make jumps into unknown territory. Leaping for a tree or branch with smooth bark they may fail to obtain a grip and tumble to the ground. Often collisions with thin twigs leave a young squirrel hanging comically by one or two feet, reaching desperately for more secure footing.

It is at this age that young squirrels are most likely to be found by humans and labeled as orphans. Perhaps the mother has indeed been killed, but more often the youngster has simply wandered too far from home. At daybreak it is stranded, cowering in a tree. If the pup escapes the notice of crows, hawks, snakes, or myriad other hungry forest dwellers, the safety of the nest is usually regained at evening when its siblings noisily emerge to resume exploring. If it recognizes the surrounding terrain, the youngster may gather the courage to make a dash for home in broad daylight.

When the squirrel is seven weeks of age, jumps begin to resemble glides, albeit clumsy and inefficient ones. Watching their early efforts one gains the impression they enjoy gliding, seeming almost excited by the realization of their ability. Practice makes perfect and young flying squirrels are diligent pupils. Once established, a good route is used over and over, glide following glide, sometimes for thirty or forty minutes without ceasing. Proficiency improves dramatically and soon the squirrels are skipping deftly along tree branches, launching into graceful arcs.

When eight weeks old, young squirrels display the bravado and self-confidence typical of adolescence. Each explores independently and the tree may seem alive with squirrels investigating every branch or practicing glides. With strident chirps and chitterings they chase each other and play in the forest canopy.

Like many young mammals, their curiosity and lack of wariness often betray their presence. Walking slowly and quietly through a forest one night near the home of a flying squirrel family, I was "greeted" by a juvenile that swooped past so close I could feel the cool turbulence. Landing on a nearby tree trunk it boldly inspected me for a long moment before continuing on its way.

Moving along, I froze to a standstill minutes later upon hearing leaves rustling a few meters above my head. The frantic sound of scraping claws was followed by a second of silence, and then a soft thump as a young squirrel landed ignominiously at my feet. In its eagerness to inspect this strange creature invading its nighttime domain, the juvenile lost its foothold and tumbled to the ground. Such unexpected falls are common throughout the life of a flying squirrel, but it merely spreads its patagium and alights unharmed on the forest floor. This particular juvenile hopped back to the tree, angrily scolding as if the embarrassing fall were my fault.

Once young squirrels are proficient gliders, the family forages as a loosely knit group because mother can no longer leave them behind. This occurs during early June in my woodlot, and parties of squirrels can sometimes be seen or heard moving through the darkness. With luck, the mother introduces her offspring to my feeding station and photographic opportunities abound for the next few weeks.

On the feeding platform, siblings feed side by side, but jump away at the slightest disturbance. Sometimes they chase about, stealing food from each other. Angry squeals and chatter accompany such encounters, but no one is ever hurt.

In the flying squirrel's behavioral repertoire, anger or displeasure is communicated by rapidly stamping the hindfeet and jerking the tail upward. These movements must be carefully orchestrated and a young squirrel's first efforts are sometimes amusing to witness. A juvenile soon discovers that stamping the hindfeet while hanging downward, suspended by those same appendages, is likely to result in an undignified tumble to the ground. Likewise, the youngster must take care when stamping on top of a limb. Unless done without lateral movement, the consequences can be equally disastrous.

An adult northern flying squirrel introduces her offspring to the feeding platform.

By twelve weeks of age, molting of the juvenile pelage begins and will be completed within a few weeks. The transformation from juvenile to subadult attire is quite painless. The entire pelt is renewed with the tail being molted last. Indeed, the condition of the tail is a good indication of the animal's youth. Juvenile tails are thin and wispy compared to the beautiful, thick tails of adults. Light easily passes through the sparse fur so flesh and bone stand out in stark silhouette. Its underside lacks the rich, creamy color acquired in adulthood.

Although now capable of surviving on their own the young remain with the mother, sharing her nest as long as she allows. However, by late June she may again accept the attentions of interested males and as her second gestation progresses she becomes increasingly less tolerant of her offspring. When time arrives to give birth, she has either driven them from the nest or moved on to a new home without them. The juveniles often remain together for several more weeks and then disperse, integrating into the surrounding flying squirrel community. When checking nestboxes I have occasionally noted that an adult male may move into the nest with the abandoned juveniles, not out of concern for them, but because their nest offers a convenient, if temporary, home.

Occasionally, an adult female nursing a litter of babies will be found sharing her nest with another grown squirrel. Where this has been observed in the wild it was not known for certain if the second animal was her offspring of an earlier litter, but this seems likely.

44

In my colony it is quite normal for a female southern flying squirrel to produce a second litter of young in midsummer. Once, while checking nestboxes, I found a female brooding five tiny, pink babies, only a few days old. Beside her, sharing the nest, was a four-month-old male from her spring litter. He was totally unconcerned about the presence of his infant half-siblings. I could not discern if he was nursing, but I did remove him from the nest. His mother had more than enough hungry mouths to feed.

Not all female southern flying squirrels produce two litters per year, but it is not unusual for older females to do so if conditions are favorable. I know of no instance where a female born in early spring gave birth to a litter later that same year. However, such a situation has been observed in red squirrels and presumably could also occur in flying squirrels. Most spring-born females do not become sexually mature until the February mating season when they are about eleven months old. A female born in late summer might mate in February when she is only six or seven months of age, if food is plentiful and winter not too stressful, but in my experience most of the late-summer females do not reproduce until they are ten to eleven months old in the following summer.

The female northern flying squirrel weans her young when they are eight to nine weeks of age, and the juveniles intently explore their surroundings. Foraging as a loosely knit group, the family shares a nest during the day. Because northern flying squirrels have only one litter per year, the female does not need to abandon or drive away her offspring in preparation for a new family. I suspect that some of the group remain together through the summer and fall, forming the nucleus of a winter aggregation. Other individuals undoubtedly leave the family group before winter, dispersing into adjacent areas or falling victim to ever-hungry predators.

Once I surreptitiously exchanged babies between three-week-old litters of southern and northern flying squirrels, giving each mother an infant of the other species. Without raising a single superciliary vibrissa (eyebrow) the females readily accepted their extra-specific charges, neatly tucking them into the nest with their own infants. The young squirrels had no difficulty adjusting. Successfully raised to weaning, they developed on the same general timetable as their litter mates.

5. *The Rites of Summer*

When juvenile flying squirrels begin actively moving about the forest after weaning, the woods can seem saturated with gliders. Being highly mobile, young squirrels can swoop long distances in a short time and every day their domain expands.

Unfortunately, life is never simple. As the squirrels enlarge their horizons, a new complication enters their lives; they must encounter the resident adult squirrels.

As it turns out, this causes more consternation for the newcomers than the older animals. Adult males and females without families tolerantly accept the young squirrels. To satisfy their curiosity, they attempt to close ranks when they first meet juveniles, but usually refrain from harassing or chasing them. If the intruder were an adult, there would be an immediate confrontation.

A young squirrel is highly agitated by its first engagement with a stranger. Instinctively assuming a defensive posture, it attempts to repel the curious adult. The pair maneuvers, keeping their bodies parallel, nose to tail. The tense juvenile stomps its back feet convulsively, tail lashing in a jerky, lateral motion. The adult noses under the juvenile's hindquarters, but is repulsed by roundhouse kicks as the young squirrel circles to keep out of reach. Quarrelsome "churring" noises are made by the juvenile. The adult eventually loses interest and moves off. After several similar episodes, the juvenile becomes less anxious and soon is accepted into the local community of gliders.

Encounters with a lactating female are more serious. A paragon of maternal virtue toward her own dependent offspring, she has no use for unfamiliar juveniles. A young squirrel wandering into her path is subject to attack. Unhesitating retreat is the best strategy.

Squirrels without family obligations are quite flexible in their activity patterns during the long, indolent summer. Finding an unused cavity or other shelter, a squirrel carries in a few green leaves, shreds them slightly to form a bed, and lounges in this parasite-free home. Or, a squirrel might share a nest with one or two other squirrels for a day. No consistent pattern is evident.

Sleepy summer days are also a good time for a change of attire. A full year's active wear and tear takes its toll on a flying squirrel's wardrobe. By midsummer the coat does not lie down with the same brilliant sheen possessed several months previously, and the dark

A summer nest of a southern flying squirrel that obviously has been snacking in bed.

The molt line is clearly evident on this squirrel's face. (NFS)

undercoat shows through in streaks and patches. Soon the pelage will be molted and replaced.

Southern flying squirrels experience a partial molt, of the head and neck only, in April and May. Males and non-lactating females start the process first; lactating females undergo the partial molt after their spring litters are three to six weeks old. Molting begins at the nose and proceeds up the face and along the cheeks. From one side of the head to the other a distinct line delimits old fur from new. Four to eight weeks are required for the change, and the molt is complete when it reaches the base of the neck.

Why this partial molt occurs is difficult to understand. Perhaps it is a vestige from an earlier time when flying squirrels had two complete molts per year, one in spring and one in autumn, as does the red squirrel. Whatever the reason, the squirrels molt again in July or August. This molt also starts at the nose and proceeds up and over the head, but does not stop at the neck. It continues down the back where the molt pattern becomes irregular. Some areas, such as the patagium, seem to shed more quickly, resulting in an uneven molt line. The tail becomes rather thin and wispy as hairs fall out, but not before new ones start growing among them. Never does it lose its flattened appearance. As before, lactating females experience this molt later, when their summer litters are close to weaning.

Northern flying squirrels that I keep in captivity seem to have only one change of pelage per year. Their thick fur somewhat obscures the molt line but in late May or June it is evident on the face, and a few weeks later the body hairs begin to shed.

It is not difficult to discern when flying squirrels are molting, even without seeing them. Entrances to tree cavities acquire a halo of gray fur and nests become lined with the soft material. The squirrels must find it somewhat annoying because the fine hairs stick to everything, getting into their eyes and mouths.

Molting and reproduction exert a large demand on the animal's energy resources, but fortunately, life is easy in summer. The exact food items available to a squirrel depend on local conditions, but summer usually provides an ample and varied smorgasbord.

Learning plays a role in what foods a squirrel will select. Captive squirrels given unfamiliar, but quite edible fare, often totally refuse it. For example, beech mast sustains flying squirrels in some forests. As many as 7 liters (7 quarts) of beechnuts have been found stashed by flying squirrels in a cavity of their winter nest tree. While visiting a beech-maple woodland I once gathered a pocketful of beechnuts for my squirrels, thinking it would be a special treat. They couldn't have been less interested; they were accustomed to the fare of an oak-hickory woodlot.

We may find the thought of eating insects repulsive, but ours is a foolish prejudice. Nutritious and tasty insects are everywhere. Squirrels eagerly eat large beetles, first discarding the hardened wing covers and legs. A family of squirrels can easily consume a liter of Junebugs at one sitting. Woodboring beetles are avidly eaten, as are grasshoppers. Grubs, larvae, and soft-bodied butterflies and moths offer additional meals. Even spiders and slugs have been noted as flying squirrel fare.

Juneberries are a gourmet squirrel's delight. The squirrels in my woods agilely climb out on branch tips searching for the ripe, red fruits. Juneberry seeds appear in their feces and are thus dispersed

Juneberries are a special treat. (SFS)

throughout the woods. Raspberries, blackberries, mulberries and other fruits are also commonly eaten by flying squirrels. Having a high water content, they are not a concentrated source of nutrients, but their sweetness is appealing. Wild black cherry trees along the edge of my woods produce abundant fruit each year, but the squirrels seem more interested in eating the contents of the pits rather than the somewhat bitter flesh of the fruit.

Nuts are not a staple summer food; most do not ripen until after the first frosts of autumn. Consequently, unless production the previous year was heavy, sprouting, deterioration, and consumption usually deplete this food source after six to nine months, and during the summer the squirrels do without. Even so, throughout late spring and early summer, I occasionally see squirrels fussing with old nut shells, perhaps extracting some of the dried contents. Examination of these shells usually shows any remaining nut meats to be black and shriveled and of doubtful nutritive value.

Nevertheless, as if impatient to obtain their favorite food, southern flying squirrels in my woodlot begin sampling the new hickory nut crop long before it ripens. Tearing nuts open, the squirrels consume them in the "milk" stage. But sometimes I wonder if the nuts are wholly palatable, because often only a portion is consumed before the nut is dropped. By the end of August the ground under a fruiting tree becomes littered with fragments of shells and partially eaten fruits from the squirrels' premature snacking.

If the crop is sparse, as is often the case where trees grow in thick stands competing for sunlight and nutrients, most of the available fruits will be removed before they have a chance to mature. This does not bode well for the coming winter. With luck, at least one species of hickory or oak will produce a crop adequate to carry the squirrels through the year's harshest season.

The diet of the northern flying squirrel generally has been regarded as similar to that of its southern relative, but this isn't an entirely valid assumption. Northern flying squirrels dwell in different ecosystems and consequently have different food resources available.

For example, the oak, hickory, and other nut trees, so important to southern flying squirrels, are primarily found in temperate deciduous forests. Geographic ranges of such trees and that of northern flying squirrels barely overlap. Nuts are consumed where they are available, but northern flying squirrels must, for the most part, do without. Native berries and insects partially fill the void.

Fungi are prime, and at certain times of the year almost exclusive, food items for northern flying squirrels. However, seldom have the squirrels been observed feeding on fungi in the wild; usually our evidence is indirect. The distinctive shape and sculpturing of fungal

An Alaskan northern flying squirrel munching on a mushroom. *Photograph by Jim W. Grace.*

A northern flying squirrel digs up a "truffle," or hypogeous fungi. *Photograph by Jim W. Grace.*

spores makes them readily identifiable under magnification. They can be detected in flying squirrel feces or the stomach contents of dead animals.

Spores found in digestive tracts of northern flying squirrels are predominantly from hypogeous fungi, those which grow underground and do not develop the fruiting bodies we commonly associate with mushrooms. Distinctive odors are emitted when the fungi mature. These attract the small mammals that dig them up to eat. Recent research has shown spores to be viable after passing through a mammalian digestive tract; thus, the animals are disseminating fungal reproductive cells through their feces.

There is another intriguing aspect to this situation. Hypogeous fungi are mycorrhizal; that is, they form a special, mutually beneficial relationship with trees. Growing as a mantle around the roots, they assist in absorption of nutrients and water while excluding harmful fungi. All our economically important tree species grow better when associated with specific mycorrhizae. Therefore, the small mammals that eat and spread these fungi become of keen interest to the forest products industry.

In the past, foresters often condemned small, seed-eating mammals because they removed large quantities of conifer seed in areas where forest managers wanted tree regeneration. Extensive and costly campaigns of broadcast poisoning were waged to eliminate rodents. Northern flying squirrels, however, are not heavy consumers of conifer seeds, contrary to some condemning literature reports. They nibble an occasional cone, and young, flushing buds are an attractive snack, but they are not staples. Even so, flying squirrels were included in the rogue's gallery of unwanted forest rodents.

In recent years, the broadcast poisoning campaigns have waned somewhat because replanting with seedlings is a more common reforestation practice. Mysteriously, some of these plantings have

Success! A *Hysterangium.*
(NFS) *Photograph by Jim W. Grace.*

failed miserably, and this failure cannot be blamed on seed-eating mammals. The explanation, we now believe, is that the carefully nurtured young trees lacked the necessary mycorrhizal fungi to grow under harsh natural conditions. Suddenly the tables are turned. The formerly condemned small mammals are vindicated; they disperse vital fungal spores through their feces. In fact, their activities may be so important for tree survival that forestry companies are developing guidelines for improving small mammal habitat in cut-over areas to encourage their wandering among the seedlings.

This squirrel-fungus relationship may also clarify an interesting account that otherwise baffled me. In 1900 Wilfred H. Osgood reported in *North American Fauna* that Alaska Indians would "not eat [flying squirrels] because the squirrels ate dirt." The Indians had probably observed the animals digging in the ground to obtain hypogeous fungi and assumed they were consuming the soil. Presumably this is also why arboreal flying squirrels regularly fall prey to terrestrial predators such as bobcats, wolves, and coyotes.

Red squirrels cut and dry fungi, caching them for later use, but evidence for northern flying squirrels doing this is almost nonexistent. It seems that fleshy hypogeous fungi would not be well preserved by such treatment. However, Darrell Hall, a graduate student at San Francisco State College, found hypogeous fungal spores in the squirrels' feces even in winter when snow depths exceeded three meters. He thought that the squirrels may have cached the fungi in an accessible spot during the previous autumn.

Though not providing a source of standing water, this jack-pine forest in the Upper Peninsula of Michigan was home for many northern flying squirrels.

Robert Mowrey, wildlife biologist with the U.S. Forest Service, radiotracked flying squirrels in Alaska. He found that they regularly visited red squirrel middens under the cover of night and pilfered the fungal caches of their diurnal relatives. In fact, the red squirrel caches seemed to be a prime element of the flying squirrel's habitat.

The northern flying squirrel's appetite for fungi was dramatically illustrated to me by my caged squirrels. Toward the end of a damp summer, fungal growth developed on the wooden structure of their large, outdoor cage. I made a mental note to paint the wood soon to protect it, but the fungi did not escape the notice of the squirrels. They began gnawing on the wood, presumably to reach the fungus mycelia, and before long some of the studs were almost cut in half.

I now provide them with fungi whenever the opportunity arises. The southern flying squirrels are indifferent, but the northern flying squirrels devour every morsel. Even the largest puffball disappears by morning.

Water requirements of flying squirrels are a topic of contention. It is often stated, or perhaps blindly repeated, that the squirrels are always found close to water, implying they cannot survive without a reliable source. When the squirrels are found some distance from an obvious water supply, stump water collecting in tree hollows is assumed to provide the requisite moisture.

However, some flying squirrels live in forests without available surface water. For example, in the southeastern United States, southern flying squirrels commonly live in oak-pine forests where water rapidly infiltrates the porous, sandy soil. Tree cavities trap moisture only temporarily and dry up after a short, rainless spell.

Alfred Avenoso of the University of Houston studied the squirrels in the xeric, long-leaf pine and turkey-oak forested sandhills of Florida where surface water was never available. These squirrels were apparently physiologically adapted to such conditions, obtaining their moisture from food, dew, and the occasional rain.

Northern flying squirrels also adjust to scarce water conditions under certain circumstances. In the Upper Peninsula of Michigan I have found them living in jack pine forests where the soil was bone dry in summer. The nearest standing water was 2 kilometers (1.2 miles) distant; surely the squirrels did not travel that far often, especially since the trip entailed crossing an expanse of open sand. Perhaps if hypogeous fungi were abundant and easily obtained throughout the summer, the squirrels got their moisture from that source. It was recently pointed out to me that the fungi are 70 percent to 80 percent water. But for now it remains a mystery how the squirrels survive without free drinking water in those habitats not providing it. When accustomed to regular access to water, the squirrels drink copiously; in this situation its availability is vital.

6. Be It Ever So Humble

Familiarity with every cavity and potential nesting site available within her home range is a must for a mother flying squirrel. Usually three to a dozen refuges can be found near a female's primary nest and she will make good use of them. While her young are growing up and dependent she quite likely will move them once or twice because of disturbance or parasites.

Jacalyn Madden noted that lactating southern flying squirrels in her New York study area changed their nest site approximately every eighteen days. Even if predators posed no problems, the regular change of location was a means of escaping infestations of fleas and other vermin that built up in the bedding. Flying squirrels are clean animals, but there are some things about which even the most fastidious mother can do nothing. Such is the case with fleas. When one home becomes too flea-ridden the family is moved to a new nest, inadvertently taking some fleas along, of course, and the cycle is started again.

As the young squirrels become independent, they also discover the locations of nearby cavities and crevices suitable for shelter. Such explorations serve a useful purpose. When danger or inclement weather threatens, a safe refuge can be reached within seconds no matter where the animal is foraging.

Some refuges are used exclusively for defecating and over the years develop a thick humus, sometimes a half-meter (20 inches) or more in depth. Other cavities, perhaps unsuitable as nesting sites for some reason, are used as feeding shelters where the squirrels can dine in comfort and safety. Inside, the remains of many meals slowly accumulate. I have found cavities in southern Michigan so full of discarded acorns and hickory nut shells that I wondered how the squirrels could even enter.

The variety, characteristics, and locations of flying squirrel nesting sites are endless. Gliders seem infinitely adept at improvising homes according to regional opportunities. Sturdy, well-insulated tree cavities are of particular importance in northern climates. Many of these result from injury and decay. Others are woodpecker excavations usurped by flying squirrels after the birds have departed.

Such homes are in heavy demand and are sought out by many different animals. Cavities harboring flying squirrels one season may later be occupied by tufted titmice, white-footed mice, red squirrels,

Cavities unsuitable as nest sites are often used as feeding shelters and fill up with discarded nut shells.

Tree cavities are prime nest sites for both species. (NFS) *Photograph by Jim W. Grace.*

bumblebees, honeybees, or many other cavity-dwellers. In my woodlot, red squirrels seem to be a chief competitor for nesting sites. One afternoon I watched as a flying squirrel was routed from its home by a red squirrel. It sailed across a clearing and disappeared into a bird house, which fortunately was not occupied at the time. The smaller squirrel often can repel such intrusions by boxing at the red squirrel as it investigates the nest entrance. However, if the red squirrel is persistent a flying squirrel is no match for it.

Antagonism sometimes occurs between flying squirrels and birds. Bird researcher David Stickel observed red-bellied woodpeckers attacking a southern flying squirrel that lived in an abandoned woodpecker hole near their new excavation. The birds started the fight and finished it. First they pulled nesting material from the hole where the squirrel slept. The drowsy mammal emerged and chased them off. The woodpeckers returned, grabbed the squirrel's tail and flung the animal from the tree for a fall of 10 meters (33 feet). The squirrel returned, but after another rude eviction, abandoned the tree cavity.

At other times compromises exist. According to naturalist John Terres, flying squirrels have been known to share their nests with white-footed mice. Audubon and Bachman recorded an old purple martin house that was taken down and found to contain about twenty flying squirrels, as many bats, and at least six screech owls. What a party!

Once it was thought that flying squirrels nested exclusively inside cavities and did not use drays, those leaf or twig nests lodged in tree cavities or crotches. However, this is not the case. Southern flying squirrels are particularly prone to use outside nests in the lower latitudes where winters are mild. Zoologist J. C. Moore reported that many of the flying squirrel nests he found in Florida were constructed outside protective cavities and, where abundant, Spanish moss was a preferred nesting material.

Most complex of the drays Moore found were those consisting of short, thin, leafy twigs woven into a sphere. Usually the interior was lined with Spanish moss or palmetto fibers, although some nests were unlined. In one case a squirrel nest was composed of dried pine needles. Drays usually were close to the tree with the opening next to the trunk.

Floridian squirrels know how to keep cool; Moore also found them residing inside the well-ventilated streamers of Spanish moss. He located these homes by looking up at the streamers backlit by sunlight. Nests were evident as dark patches within the mass of vegetation. Sometimes the squirrels merely pushed the moss aside to form a chamber, but other streamer nests consisted of a ball of dried moss suspended within the rootless epiphyte.

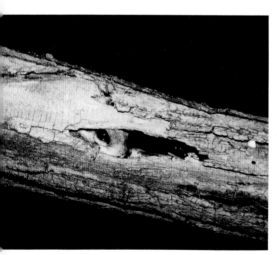

Every possible crevice is investigated. (SFS)

Large, old trees frequently offer excellent home sites.

Fox squirrel leaf nests, or drays, are sometimes used by southern flying squirrels.

Records of outside nests are less common in the northern portion of the species' range. Occasionally southern flying squirrels are found living in drays, but not, to the best of my knowledge, during winter. A variety of materials is used to construct the drays, such as shredded bark, twigs, leaves, or sphagnum moss. I have never found a flying squirrel dray; according to literature sources, they resemble fox squirrel drays, but are smaller, about 20 centimeters (8 inches) in diameter.

Southern flying squirrels do not object to using abandoned fox or gray squirrel drays, either constructing their nest on top of the structure, or creating a nest chamber in the mass of leaves and twigs. Use of this type of shelter seems to occur throughout the range of the southern flying squirrel, wherever it coexists with these larger squirrel species. Flying squirrels also have been known to build homes on abandoned bird nests.

Unlikely though it may seem for arboreal species, both southern and northern flying squirrels have been unearthed from subterranean nests. For example, Moore disturbed a flying squirrel from a tree nest and it glided to the ground, disappearing into a hole near the base of a pine stump. A bit of excavating revealed that this hole connected to a pocket gopher tunnel. Under a nearby stump was a sphagnum moss nest containing gray fur, apparently that of a flying squirrel.

In another instance, a surveyor overturned a log, exposing a rather surprised northern flying squirrel with her litter of four young. Biologist E. A. Mearns wrote of finding a nest at the root of a chestnut tree. It contained a female and her five young, which she immediately removed to a nest tree.

Northern flying squirrels frequently use drays. Biologist Ian McTaggart Cowan described two categories of exterior nests from British Columbia. Both types contained soft bark or lichens; larger nests were completely encased in twigs and branches while smaller ones were simply built on platforms of twigs. Cowan concluded that drays were preferred for summer nests while tree cavities were used in winter.

Robert Mowrey has found Alaskan northern flying squirrels nesting in the massive "witches' brooms" of white spruce trees infested with rust disease. The brooms are large, 0.5–1 meter (20–40 inches) in diameter, and the animals weave nesting material into the thick tangle of branches creating a secure chamber. These abodes seem to be preferred over other types of nests, and are used in winter when the squirrels aggregate.

On the other hand, while working in the Sierra Nevada, Darrell Hall discerned a seasonal pattern in the use of brooms and other nesting sites by northern flying squirrels. In summer, the squirrels used witches' brooms most frequently, along with some drays, but only a few cavities. As the autumn rains began the squirrels started using cavities more, although they continued to reside in brooms as well. By winter, the squirrels had mainly shifted to natural cavities in large, live fir trees and to some woodpecker excavations. They did not return to the brooms until spring.

Zoologist H. J. Rust described northern flying squirrel nests in Idaho "constructed of dry grass blades and lined with lichens and fastened to the bole of the tree and to a supporting limb at heights varying from 12 to 15 feet." Zoologist Vernon Bailey found squirrel nests in the sheets and streamers of moss draping trees in the mountains of Oregon. To reach these nests the squirrels had made "well-worn trails up the trunks and along the larger branches."

As shown by these and many other written accounts, flying squirrels are quite flexible in their nesting requirements, and each animal is well-acquainted with all the available shelters within its range. Their propensity for exploring would have gladdened the hearts of Lewis and Clark. Any rearrangement within the woodland, such as a windthrown tree or new woodpecker excavation, is quickly discovered and investigated. After a thorough reconnaissance, the squirrel memorizes details of the new situation and has no trouble returning to the exact spot.

Squirrels routinely follow specific, well-established gliding routes between sheltering sites. When disturbed from their daytime retreats, they almost invariably use the same pathway to escape to a nearby snag. Not bothering to look before they leap, the squirrels instead rely upon memory to take a safe pathway. As Jacalyn Madden commented:

> . . . the rhythm of muscular actions involved in getting from one point to another by a particular route may be memorized and then rigidly, even blindly,

In some areas, red squirrels are competitors for nest sites.

followed although this is not necessarily the most direct or easiest route between those points.

Illar Muul removed a snag that a group of squirrels regularly used for escape and found that they still tried to glide to it without first looking. One squirrel made four attempts, from different angles, to land on the missing tree snag before finally taking refuge elsewhere.

Muul used this behavior pattern to advantage when capturing squirrels for his research. Upon disturbing a nest of sleeping squirrels he noted the escape route of the first animal. Then carrying a large net, he took a stance near the landing site while his assistant dislodged another squirrel. Like a determined kamikaze, it used the same route and was scooped up in the net as it glided past Muul.

7. Life Is One Damned Thing After Another

Life is precarious for flying squirrels, and, in most cases, short. Captive animals often live ten to thirteen years, but by that age teeth are worn out and bones are distorted by arthritis. Mercifully, wild squirrels rarely live long enough to suffer such afflictions. Occasionally a squirrel survives more than four or five years; most end their brief lives as a predator's dinner or succumb to the elements.

Owls are major predators of flying squirrels. Unlike mammals, these birds can pursue gliding squirrels through the air, their silent flight often undetected until it is too late for the squirrel to take evasive action. Once while watching a flying squirrel at my feeder, I glimpsed a great horned owl swoop past only a meter away. Its stealth and large size sent a cold chill up my spine, yet its intended prey remained oblivious, never pausing even a moment from its meal. Had my presence not deterred it, the owl easily would have caught the squirrel. Barn owls, barred owls, long-eared owls, and spotted owls are other known predators of flying squirrels, although probably any owl species will seize one if the opportunity presents itself.

Flying squirrels are especially important prey for the spotted owl of western North America. At least half its diet consists of flying squirrels and a pair of owls might consume 500 squirrels annually. In fact, as a prime item on the owl's menu, the northern flying squirrel has become embroiled in a hot political issue. The diverse, old-growth conifer forests where the squirrels and owls reside are rapidly being harvested. Although the squirrels are in no danger of extinction, the owls are declining in numbers. The current debate is over how much old growth should be preserved to maintain viable owl populations. The solution will affect not only the owls but also the squirrels upon which they depend as prey.

Flying squirrels certainly recognize owls as potential threats. Owl hoots can start a southern flying squirrel angrily chirping. However, a resident owl by no means portends the certain demise of flying squirrels in the nearby woods. J. C. Moore found flying squirrel bones in owl pellets under a great horned owl nest, yet concluded that the birds were having little impact on the overall squirrel population. At least fifteen additional squirrels lived within 100 meters (330 feet)

Owls are major predators of flying squirrels. (Screech owl, *Otus asio*)

of the owl nest.

When Jacalyn Madden examined owl pellets at her Long Island study site she found plenty of bones from young rabbits and rats, but none from flying squirrels, although they were abundant that year. She kept an eye on pairs of great horned owls nesting near squirrel hideouts, yet the birds never paid attention to the gliders.

Red-tailed hawks, although diurnal predators, also eat some flying squirrels. A study of these birds by S. Luttich and his associates in Alberta showed that about 1 percent of the birds' diet consisted of northern flying squirrels. Unfortunately, the authors did not explain how the hawks captured the nocturnal prey, but presumably their activity periods overlapped at dawn or dusk.

Then there are the mammalian predators. Flying squirrel remains have been found in the stomach contents and scats of bobcats, lynxes, and even wolves. Coyotes, foxes, and skunks are known to eat them as well. Weasels take a toll; their sinuous bodies easily enter tree cavities harboring gliders, and only a flying leap can save the squirrel. Some trappers claim that pine martens are most readily found in regions supporting an abundant flying squirrel population, implying that the squirrels are preferred prey. A survey of marten scats in the Sierra Nevada showed flying squirrels contributed 10 percent of the predator's winter diet.

Near farms and residential areas, domestic cats are deadly predators. Even pampered, well-fed house pets cannot resist stalking them. In 1956 G. C. Toner of Haliburton, Ontario, wrote in the *Journal of Mammalogy* that cats frequently captured northern flying squirrels and brought their victims home to consume, leaving nothing but the squirrels' thick, furry tails as evidence of their depredations.

The fragile tail is easily broken off. (NFS)

A flying squirrel that lacks part of its tail is not an unusual sight. Being rather fragile, the tail breaks easily and may be lost in a close encounter with a predator. It might hurt, but such an amputation has probably saved the lives of countless squirrels.

Squirrels also survive the loss of entire limbs, as illustrated by the handicapped squirrel reported by squirrel researcher, Fred Barkalow. This animal lacked a tail and a left hind foot, yet foraged successfully and was in good health at the time Barkalow shot it. Perhaps it lost its lower leg to a predator or, more likely to a shotgun blast; the squirrel was frequenting a pecan grove, a place where its kind are not welcome.

Predation by snakes is common in southern states. Slithering through the trees, the reptiles silently enter nests to capture the occupants. This may be one reason why the squirrels prefer nesting in masses of Spanish moss during the summer snake season. A tree cavity usually offers only one exit; a mass of vegetation is less confining, and the squirrel can burst out in any direction, if necessary.

Biologist P. G. Pearson came upon a Florida rat snake that was in the process of swallowing a flying squirrel. He intervened, releasing the squirrel from the snake's deadly grip, and it escaped up a nearby tree unharmed. Timber rattlers and black snakes are also known to prey upon flying squirrels.

To me, the most unusual account of predation on a flying squirrel was recorded by naturalist Ernest T. Seton. He found a hapless squirrel in the stomach of a trout. Flying squirrels cannot swim swiftly; presumably this one fell into the stream and was an easy strike for the fish. More imaginatively, Seton speculated that the fish magnificently leaped to catch the squirrel as it glided low over the water's surface.

Drowning is not an uncommon demise for flying squirrels but contrary to the claims of some authors, they can swim. However, the patagium dangerously hinders their strokes. Unless the squirrel can paddle its way to safety within a few minutes, it is soon exhausted.

In the past, flying squirrels often drowned in sap buckets during maple sugar time, driven to their death by a craving for the sugary fluid at a time of year when food is scarce. Fortunately, modern sap buckets are usually covered, preventing animals and unwanted debris from contaminating the sap.

Open water tanks and cisterns present another hazard. Biologist W. L. McAtee recalled living in a house shared by flying squirrels. Before he screened off the water supply, squirrels frequently fell in and drowned. He claimed to have become expert in detecting a change in the water's taste, indicating it was time to remove another dead flying squirrel. Livestock water tanks on farms also can be deathtraps. An easy remedy is to lean a stick or board into the water so the squirrels can climb out.

Even the flying squirrels' spectacular mode of locomotion has risks. They occasionally strike objects in mid-air despite their excellent night vision. While preparing a dead squirrel for a museum specimen, Robert Wrigley of Winnipeg, Manitoba, discovered a curious encapsulated structure under the skin of the animal's chest. On further inspection it proved to be a winter bud of balsam poplar. Wrigley surmised that the squirrel had lodged the bud under its skin while gliding. No inflammation was present around the foreign object. Wrigley pointed out that balsam poplar produces a sticky resin that is commercially extracted as a soothing skin ointment. The bud,

Open-top maple sap buckets can be death traps for squirrels that fall in while trying to drink the sweet fluid.

saturated with oil, served to prevent inflammation and promoted healing around itself.

Hard-to-see strands of barbed wire pose a threat because the squirrels may become entangled. In the Upper Peninsula of Michigan, zoologist James Findley found a dead female, trapped by a barb. The edge of her left patagium was caught on it, and, in trying to escape, she further entrapped herself, fighting until exhausted. Both front incisors were broken in her attempts to bite through the wire.

Bird-banders and bat-trapping mammalogists present a novel hazard. They stretch thin, almost invisible nylon nets across forest openings to catch animals for research, but sometimes a hapless flying squirrel glides into the web instead. Usually the squirrel can be removed from the net and released unharmed, but I suspect it ever after suffers nightmares of giant, squirrel-eating spiders.

As do all wild animals, flying squirrels of both species harbor a diverse array of internal and external parasites. Fleas are the most prominent of these and virtually every animal has some; more than a dozen species have been found on flying squirrels. Mites and lice may parasitize flying squirrels but are not as ubiquitous as the fleas. A tick can usually be removed by a squirrel before it becomes attached unless it is on top of the head or between the shoulder blades. Then it is able to retain its grip and engorge with blood. The only thing the squirrel can do is endure and wait for it to drop off. Internal parasites of flying squirrels include flatworms, roundworms, and protozoa.

Parasites are irritating, but rarely do they alone cause the death of the host. Usually only under stressful conditions such as food shortages do parasites significantly contribute to the host's demise.

Mortality from disease is difficult to monitor in flying squirrel populations. An ailing squirrel quickly falls prey to a predator, which removes the evidence, or quietly dies in a secluded and inaccessible tree cavity. Only occasionally do we glimpse infirmities in wild squirrels.

Rabies is undoubtedly the most sensationalized disease of wild and domestic animals, but only three cases have been reported in flying squirrels. Afflicted squirrels do not swoop from the trees to attack people. However, if found, they do not attempt to escape in the manner of healthy animals.

The first recorded case of rabies in flying squirrels occurred in Florida in 1961. Three boys were fishing along a canal north of St. Petersburg one afternoon when a flying squirrel fell out of a nearby tree. It did not attempt to escape and was caught and taken to the boys' home, where it bit two of them while being handled. The next day it died. An examination for rabies was positive.

A more recent case involved ten-year-old Crispin Susan Reedy of Auburn, Alabama, in 1978. Crispin related her experience to me in a letter:

> I live in a rather thickly wooded residential area which has mainly tall pines. When the squirrel was first found it was not moving. We thought it had been injured so I picked it up, to see if I could help it, and it bit me. It dragged itself in a zigzag manner for several yards before I caught it by scooping it up in a box. It [the brain tissue] was examined by the flourescent antibody technique which found the presence of rabies antigen.

With treatment, Crispin survived with no ill effects. However, both accounts emphasize the importance of not handling injured or seemingly sick wild animals without taking proper precautions.

Recently, another disease, potentially transmissible to humans, was identified in southern flying squirrels. Throughout history, epidemic typhus has been associated with humans, the infection being carried by body lice. Although the disease-causing organism, *Rickettsia prowazekii*, has been identified in livestock ticks, animals were thought to be an unimportant reservoir for the human disease.

In the early 1960s, serological tests on wild flying squirrels in Virginia and several other eastern states revealed that a high percentage of the animals were infected with the rickettsia. An article in the 1981 *Journal of the American Medical Association (JAMA)* stated the following:

> Between July 1977 and January 1980, seven cases of sporadic, nonepidemic "Epidemic" typhus were discovered in Virginia, West Virginia, and North Carolina. . . . The reservoir seemed to be the southern flying squirrel. The disease seemed milder than classic louse-born epidemic typhus, but in some instances, it was life-threatening.

The mode of transmission from squirrel to human is unclear, but may be through fleas or lice. Cases of the disease are rare but in most of those reported in *JAMA*, victims were in a situation where they could encounter parasites. For example, one woman lived in an old farmhouse with a deteriorating roof that allowed rodents easy entry. Live-trapping around the house resulted in the capture of thirty-seven flying squirrels and several other rodents. When a human contracts the disease, an epidemic does not follow. Thanks to modern hygiene, few people harbor the ectoparasites that spread the disease from human to human. Therefore, flying squirrels are not a peril to public health.

Fortunately, the situation is usually mutual. Flying squirrels normally need have little to fear from humans directly. These squirrels tend to be less wary toward us than are other wild squirrels, probably because they are nocturnal and seldom noticed or harassed. Compared to fox and gray squirrels, diminutive flying squirrels are hardly worth the trouble of hunting for the sake of the meat they offer, although it is claimed they are as palatable as the large game squirrels. Because their pelts are small and delicate, flying squirrels have no commercial value and are of little interest to trappers.

However, leghold traps can be an unintentional threat. Numerous accounts describe how dozens, sometimes hundreds, of northern flying squirrels have been caught in trap lines set for more valuable fur-bearers. Curious to learn if these reports were legitimate, I enlisted aid through the Northern Michigan Trapper's Association, asking if any of their members ever accidentally caught flying squirrels. The association officer I dealt with was rather skeptical, but willing to help and duly notified the members. At the end of winter I received word that several trappers had indeed accidentally caught the squirrels. Such incidents occurred where smaller traps for weasel or mink were used. Flying squirrels simply do not possess the heft to trigger traps set for the larger fur-bearers such as raccoons, foxes, or bobcats.

That squirrels should so readily enter traps set for carnivores may seem a bit peculiar, but during winter trapping season, hungry animals seek any food source. The bait's odor entices them.

Under such circumstances the squirrels are considered nuisances. The carcasses of squirrels accidentally trapped are either discarded or used for bait. In the past, trappers in the Adirondack Mountains claimed they often had to "clean out" the flying squirrels in some areas before the more valuable, small fur-bearers could get to the traps.

Occasionally, flying squirrels are killed by hunters. Because the squirrels sleep during the day they are usually taken only by those hunters with the unsportsmanlike habit of pounding on hollow trees to chase out their quarry. A flying squirrel disturbed from its midday sleep is so lethargic and dull that shooting it can hardly be described as sporting. But they do make an unusual and attention-diverting trophy to bring home when hunting is otherwise poor.

Fortunately, such hunters are not a serious threat to flying squirrel populations. Often squirrels refuse to leave their nests in spite of vigorous pounding, or the den is so high that the disturbance receives little notice. Many weekend hunters are unaware that flying squirrels even exist. When questioning hunters about flying squirrels, I find only the more experienced and serious of them have any knowledge of the animals. Casual hunters are apt to react to my questions with suspicion, as if I were trying to pull a fast one. Flying squirrels, indeed! Only in the *Rocky and Bullwinkle* cartoon.

8. A Little Flying Squirrel, With Batlike Wings

No matter how often I witness the deft glides of flying squirrels in action, fascination and envy linger. Their beauty, grace, and efficiency of locomotion defy description. Watching them is one of the most delightfully entertaining activities I know of, and I am reminded of Thomas Morton's *New English Canaan*. In 1632 he wrote of " . . . a little flying Squirrill, with bat like winges, which hee spreads when hee jumpes from tree to tree and does no harme."

Flying squirrels possess remarkable control over the speed and direction of glides even though they cannot maneuver in the manner of a free-flying bird or bat. Straight, swift glides are suitable in a forest clear of tall underbrush, but often a squirrel must swerve to avoid branches and other vegetation. This it accomplishes by a deceptively smooth swing to the left or right. Effortless it seems; no patagial movement is evident, nor sound is heard as the animal banks and turns.

Flying squirrels usually start either from a roughly horizontal surface, such as a branch, or while hanging head downward on a tree trunk. If necessary, the agile glider can launch itself from virtually any position, even executing a backward somersault and twist to become airborne.

On a familiar gliding route the squirrel simply leaps out and spreads the patagium with no other preparation. However, an inexperienced young squirrel, or one about to embark on an unfamiliar route, displays more caution and looks before it leaps. Bobbing up and down in a rapid series of "push-ups," or leaning far left and right in rapid succession, the squirrel studies its prospective gliding path. If still not satisfied, it scurries sideways, crablike, for a better view from a different angle.

Presumably, such bobbing gymnastics allow better judgment of relative position and distance through parallax. As in most rodents, the flying squirrel's eyes are placed far to the sides of the head, providing a wide field of vision, good for detecting predators coming from any direction. However, such eye placement also restricts the field of visual overlap to the front and therefore limits depth perception. The squirrel's small head, with only a short distance between

Poetry in motion.

the eyes, further accentuates the problem. To overcome these limitations a squirrel triangulates, viewing its glide path from two or more angles, each as far from the other as possible.

A navigational fix taken, the squirrel crouches low. Powerful hindlegs launch the intrepid aeronaut. Once the squirrel is airborne, it spreads its patagium to control speed and direction of descent. However, sometimes it allows itself to plummet several breathless meters with legs held close to the body before opening the patagium like a parachute to abruptly interrupt the fall. It then planes off on its glide path.

Thin, flat muscles lie within the gliding skin, serving to control movement of the airfoil. Along the outer edge of the patagium strong, ropelike muscles hold the skin edge taut during a glide. Additional muscles stabilize the outstretched legs. When not in use, the patagium is held loosely against the animal's sides by still another set of muscles, preventing interference with movement while the squirrel is afoot.

Also within the folds of skin, lying parallel to the forearm, is a slender, cartilaginous rod attached at one end to the wrist. Called the styliform cartilage, this rod extends away from the forearm during a glide, serving to further open the leading edge of the gliding surface.

Seen from below, a gliding squirrel resembles a kite
with a broad tail.

While the squirrel glides, its flattened tail merely trails behind,
flowing out with a slight curve to the left or right, or with the tip
flapping from side to side like a flag blown by a gentle breeze. The
tail's function during a glide is not fully understood, but referring to
it as a rudder is misleading. The tail does not control glide direction.
More accurately, it serves as a balancing organ, similar to the tail of
a kite, stabilizing the glider in midair. In addition, its large surface
area increases the squirrel's total airfoil. In some large northern flying
squirrels the tail may contribute 20 percent to 30 percent of the
gliding surface. Should it be lost through accident or injury, the
squirrel quickly learns to compensate for its absence. Many wild
squirrels glide deftly with tail portions missing.

Photographs of squirrels in flight show the facial whiskers pro-
jected forward, a position that keeps them away from the outstretched forelegs. The suggestion has been put forth that holding
the tactilely sensitive whiskers in this attitude helps the animal
steer clear of obstacles in the glide path, because it receives warning
of an object's presence an instant before impact. That a squirrel could
swerve so abruptly at the last possible moment seems unlikely,
because the whiskers would provide only a fraction of a second's
warning. Nevertheless, such contact might give it at least a chance
to flinch or duck its head, offering some protection to the eyes. In

Feet are spread wide to fully open the patagium.

the same way, the long flexible whiskers might provide last moment information about the landing site, allowing the squirrel to antici- pate, for instance, where its feet will touch down. Squirrels often shut their eyes protectively an instant before landing, perhaps in response to what they feel through the whiskers.

Richard Thorington of the Smithsonian Institution and Lawrence Heaney of The University of Michigan discerned a remarkable simi- larity between the squirrels and certain Rogalo-wing hang gliders having an aspect ratio (length to breadth) of 1.5 with a wing loading of 1 pound per square foot. Flying squirrels seem to have a maximum gliding ratio (horizontal distance to vertical drop) of 3, similar to the hang glider. This represents an angle of descent of about 30° with the horizon. Light in weight, flying squirrels have low wing loading and, as gliders, do not "penetrate" the air well, being vulnerable to tur- bulence. Thorington and Heaney noted, "lightly loaded flying squir- rels are best adapted to gliding in forested areas where there is little turbulence and where slow flight speed and high maneuverability are important."

Camber (curvature) of the airfoil affects the squirrel's glide ratio and is controlled by the muscles sandwiched in the patagial skin. A flat airfoil allows the squirrel to glide swiftly and for a long distance. If this billow is less than 1°, sideslipping becomes a danger, but it is doubtful if a squirrel could ever flatten its patagium to such an extent.

The styliform cartilage at the wrist assists in opening the patagium even further.

A billow of 3°–4° is normal for a hang glider, and presumably a flying squirrel as well, although no one has ever measured the amount of camber of an airborne squirrel.

Illar Muul and John Alley described the squirrel's maneuverability in the air:

> Direction of the glide is determined by manipulation of the forearms. For example, a left turn is accomplished by dropping the left arm lower than the right. This creates aerodynamic drag against the right membrane and the squirrel is spun into a turn. Several turns are sometimes made in rapid succession, and there is little doubt that such fancy aerobatics come in handy when the squirrel is being chased by its most common nocturnal enemy, the owl.

A squirrel's posture is dynamic through a flight. According to Thorington and Heaney:

> The initial part of the glide is steep and probably represents the period of time when the squirrel is reaching optimal velocity for gliding. Having reached this velocity, the squirrel is able to flatten out its glide to maximize the horizontal distance covered. At the end of the flight, it increases the angle of attack, which may cause it to swoop upwards before landing.

During this upward swing, a meter or two before landing, the patagium billows like a parachute to reduce speed. All four legs swing forward; front feet touch the tree an instant before the hind feet.

Preparing to land, the squirrel assumes a more upright posture and brings its feet to the front.

Except for the sound of sturdy, curved claws grasping bark, the landing is almost soundless, a fitting end for a silent glide through the forest.

Many variations from the "normal" gliding procedure are displayed. Takeoffs occur from nearly any position, and occasionally do so accidentally after a squirrel loses its footing. Sometimes it fails to notice an obstacle and gets knocked for a loop halfway through a glide; thin electrical and telephone wires are a particular hazard in this respect. However, the squirrel quickly recovers its composure and twists back into gliding position before hitting the ground.

A glide can be a downward spiral instead of a horizontal movement. To drop straight down a squirrel pancakes with the patagium outspread, landing spread-eagled on all four feet.

In crossing short distances of 3 meters (10 feet) or less, a squirrel may end up higher than it started, propelled by a strong thrust from its hindlegs. Altitude is always lost on longer glides. To continue traveling through the forest the animal must ascend the landing tree to a height sufficient to leap into the next glide. Repeating this sequence several times along familiar gliding paths, the squirrel can cover considerable distances rapidly. I dare you to try keeping up on the ground below!

Once in the air, the squirrels are adept pilots. Squirrel researcher Dwight Sollberger wrote:

Many glides are initiated from a head downward position. (SFS)

Turns of more than 90° were observed on many occasions. In one instance the animal was observed to glide down a steep slope for approximately 75 feet [23 meters]. It then turned at right angles to its former direction and glided parallel to the slope, finally turning and landing on a tree on the slope slightly above the lowest point of its glide. The total distance covered in this glide could not have been less than 125 feet [38 meters].

Most glides are for distances of 6 to 20 meters (20 to 60 feet) as the squirrel forages through the canopy. However, there is no such thing as a typical glide. Any distance within the ability of the animal may be covered. Watching squirrels in my woods, I sometimes catch sight of one gliding and can follow it, visually, for some distance. But they are elusive creatures. The dense tree stand and undergrowth often prevent me from seeing either where the squirrel started or where it landed, and sometimes both. So often, my sightings are merely glimpses of a small form flitting through an opening in the tree canopy. I just happen to be looking at the right place at the right, brief moment.

The maximum distance squirrels are capable of gliding is always an intriguing question. Audubon and Bachman wrote of squirrels gliding 45 meters (150 feet) from the top of an oak. Sollberger observed one glide of more than 46 meters (152 feet) from a height of 18 meters (60 feet). The record for long glides was provided by zoologist A. Brooker Klugh who watched a squirrel jump from a stub and sail down a mountainside for more than 92 meters (300 feet)—the length of a football field. Squirrel-watcher Laura Heinold almost matched this observation when she measured a glide that started in a tall oak and covered 88 meters (285 feet) over a sloping hillside.

Some people have reported hearing chirps and chittering sounds as the squirrels glide, and have speculated on the purpose of these vocalizations. Bats emit high-pitched sounds for aerial echolocation and, of course, it was inevitable that someone would suggest that flying squirrels do the same.

Using electronic monitoring devices, Jacalyn Madden recorded vocalizations made during glides, noting that these sounds were also made by young squirrels just learning to glide. Audible to human ears, they had some ultrasonic components and were emitted in short pulses. However, she was unable to establish if the animals indeed used echolocation.

The highly specialized hearing ability necessary for echolocation, as found in bats, is not possessed by flying squirrels. The only feature of this nature that differs significantly from other squirrel species is the inflated ear cavity, an adaptation for increased sound reception. A valuable asset for a nocturnal animal under any circumstances, it is not necessarily associated with echolocation ability.

Although flying squirrels apparently do not rely upon echolocation for gliding safely through a darkened forest, at least to the extent that bats do, their excellent sense of hearing must undoubtedly enable them to gather a great deal of information about their environment. Many mammals, such as whales, seals, shrews, tenrecs, dormice, hamsters, and others, are known to use their keen hearing ability to locate articles they cannot see. Even blind humans who have a highly trained sense of hearing sometimes can detect objects through elementary echolocation. Flying squirrels could have similar ability.

Flying squirrels emit other vocalizations not associated with gliding. Birdlike chirping, often described as a "tsepp, tsepp," is the most commonly heard sound of the southern flying squirrel. After a person learns to recognize this distinctive chirp it is unmistakable. Countless times I have detected the presence of squirrels in a woodlot before even seeing them, simply because I heard their calling.

The "tsepp" is an alarm call. Predators, a strange noise, or a human walking through the woods may cause a squirrel to voice it. The animal scurries to a high, safe perch and may continue calling, every one to four seconds, for five to ten minutes without ceasing. Mouth opened wide to emit the sound, the squirrel heaves with effort. Can a squirrel be said to look worried or anxious? If so, then that is exactly how I describe its expression and attitude. Locating the source of the call in the forest is difficult. Piercing and distinct, the sound diffuses through the woods without betraying the squirrel's hiding spot.

The patagium in no way hinders a squirrel when it is afoot. (SFS)

Northern flying squirrels have no comparable vocalization. A "chucking" is their chief sound. Sometimes coming as a slow series of "chuck, chuck, chuck" notes, it is not as loud or piercing as the southern flying squirrel's "tsepp," and is difficult to detect farther than 10 meters (33 feet) from the source.

When a squirrel of either species is scampering away from a threatening situation it will often utter a rapid sequence of chatters that slur together into what I call "chittering." This sound is issued only once or twice, then the squirrel reverts to the alarm call typical of its species.

Madden described a snorting sound made by dominant southern flying squirrels when threatening another squirrel. When fighting or scuffling, flying squirrels emit harsh squeals and squawks. These are also heard when a predator or human invades the nest, putting the animals on the defensive. When reaching into a nest of sleeping squirrels, I often feel fortunate that I am unable to translate these squirrelese complaints. They would surely be unprintable!

These vocalizations are commonly heard in the wild. The quieter, subtle sounds emitted by flying squirrels are usually only heard by humans when the squirrels are kept in captivity. Anyone with a pet squirrel soon comes to appreciate the wide range of soft, expressive sounds it will make.

For instance, a squirrel investigating an object, quietly snuffles through its nose. If that object is dusty, the exploration ends with one or two sneezes and a thorough washing of the face accompanied by little sputtering noises. Sitting back on its haunches enjoying a scrap of food, a squirrel may emit a quiet humming chatter, as if warning anyone nearby to leave it alone; it will not share its meal.

Northern flying squirrels often chortle quietly to themselves as they move about examining things. Females of this species sometimes quietly mutter to their offspring in the nest, perhaps reassuring them. In general, northern flying squirrels tend to be less vocal than their southern relatives, but I find them more expressive in the few sounds they do make. Tame squirrels will often climb onto my shoulder, conversationally "chuck, chuck, chucking" all the while as if to convey some profound sciurid sentiment. If only I could understand!

9. He That Would Eat the Kernel Must First Crack the Nut

Nuts in my woodlot are finally ripening when autumn arrives. By day, red squirrels and fox squirrels search far out onto branch tips, seemingly inviting a disastrous fall. Even chipmunks occasionally clamber up into the lower branches to collect a meal. Flying squirrels continue the hunt after dark.

The seasonally changing day length has a discernible effect on the southern flying squirrels' behavior; it brings out their hoarding instinct. Activity increases frantically; food storing becomes almost frenzied. As squirrel owner F. H. King stated in rather colorful prose a century ago, "The circumstances were such that the acorns awakened a new and intense emotion which in an instant seemed to fill his whole being to overflowing. . . ."

Illar Muul studied this behavior change in the laboratory, placing groups of squirrels under different light and temperature regimes. Photoperiod, independent of temperature, was found to be the cue for increased storing behavior. Nut hoarding increased under light conditions typical of early October in southern Michigan, and remained at a high level until the light was equivalent to early January. Squirrels kept months out of phase with the natural cycle displayed increased storing behavior only when the light was equivalent to that of October.

By lengthening the light period from nine to fifteen hours, Muul was able to drastically reduce hoarding by 50 percent within six days. This change in photoperiod was a condensed version of what occurs in the winter months, when caching almost ceases.

Muul's experiments demonstrated that storing behavior in the laboratory is dictated by light, not temperature. But what happens in a lab is not always exactly what happens in the wild. While observing southern flying squirrels in my woodlot I have noted that weather has a definite effect on their activity. Although light conditions ignite the urge to store food, weather may modify it. Heavy wind and rainfall can make the squirrels reluctant to venture out. Also, during the first few nights that temperatures drop below freezing, the squirrels are slow to emerge from the nest, like a swimmer afraid to enter cold water. All this puts a damper on their storing activity, but a few weeks later, when such temperatures are the rule, the squirrels have adjusted and busily gather nuts regardless.

Autumn is my favorite time for squirrel watching. The woods are a special place at this time of the year. Mosquitoes no longer pester, and the crisp leaf litter betrays movements of everything equally, from the small, white-footed mouse to the sleek, fat doe with her two half-grown offspring. Flying squirrels no longer demurely retire when I enter the woods. Instead, after gaining a safe perch, they loudly "tsepp" at me.

If I am as unobtrusive as possible, the squirrels are not agitated for long. Soon I'll see a dark form gliding from tree to tree. In the quiet, a flying squirrel can be heard in its eager quest for nuts, climbing nimbly to the far ends of the boughs. Farther and farther out it moves, balancing on top of the branch. As the support becomes precariously thin the squirrel topples over, continuing its mission upside down, paw over paw, like a marine in basic training. When the nut is reached, careful acrobatics are required to cut it from the tree while retaining a grip on the twig. If necessary, the squirrel can hang by hindfeet alone, its curved claws serving as grappling hooks while front feet remove and manipulate the nut.

If a hickory nut is the prize, its shucks are torn off; an acorn has its cap removed. These discarded bits clatter to the ground. Several squirrels working together in a heavily laden tree can produce a veritable cascade of fragments.

The ability to balance atop a precariously thin support is useful for finding food in a treetop. (NFS)

Before the nut can be stored, the husks must be removed.

A notch is cut at one end . . .

providing a handle for carrying the nut.

A southern flying squirrel harvests a nut.

A few ripe nuts break loose as squirrels move through the branches, and these also drop noisily, caroming off branches and foliage on their way to the ground. Later the squirrels search for the fallen nuts. Scuffling through dry leaves they seem to have little regard for the racket they make; if danger threatens, a tree trunk is never more than a few bounds away.

Without doubt, hickory nuts are the favorite food of southern flying squirrels. Even naïve, young squirrels seem to know instinctively how to handle these nuts like pros upon their first encounter. Peter Weigl of Wake Forest University compared the geographic range of southern flying squirrels with the limits of the hickories and pecans; the match is close but not perfect. Hickories cover a major portion of the species' range but are lacking at extremes of the squirrels' distribution. In these areas, acorns probably become the important food resource and perhaps are vital to the animals' survival. Where hickory nuts are not available, southern flying squirrel populations suffer dramatically during poor acorn years.

Southern flying squirrels follow a definite procedure when processing hickory nuts for storage, although each squirrel shows individual variation in technique. After finding a nut, either cutting it from a tree or salvaging it from the ground, the squirrel removes the heavy, green husk to expose the woody nut shell. How easily this is accomplished varies. Some hickories have nuts with thin, loose husks that almost drop away. Others have tight, thick husks that do not readily split open. Often these husks must be cut away bit by bit at great effort.

Once this is done, a squirrel can distinguish almost immediately whether the nut is a good one or if the contents are dried and worthless. Often this can be discerned even before the husk is removed; the weight of the nut relative to its volume being the vital clue. No

A suitable spot is located for burial . . .   then a small hole is dug.

time is wasted; the unacceptable nut is summarily discarded and the squirrel sets off in search of another. On the other hand, a nut that seems satisfactory is deftly rotated in the forepaws while the squirrel "feels" it by scraping with the incisors. This gives an even better sounding of the nut's quality. A wormy nut may have the proper weight but the contents are no longer firm; a different resonance betrays its occupants. It takes only a few seconds to sort out the bad fruits.

Passing inspection, the nut is ready for storage. Holding it in its forepaws, the squirrel uses its lower incisors to cut notches on either side of the peduncle, that stemlike structure on the nut. These notches provide a firm grip, facilitating transportation.

Exactly where squirrels store all the nuts they harvest still mystifies me. Popular imagery has squirrels caching huge hoards in hollow trees, but rarely are such caches found. Quite likely they are the exception rather than the rule. A concentrated cache of nuts is a virtual gold mine for any other animal happening upon it. Pilfering would soon deplete the store, leaving the squirrel with naught.

Instead, flying squirrels scatter-hoard, that is, they store the nuts individually in many locations, the forest floor being the most common depository. In a good nut year, with several squirrel species hard at work around the clock, the earth must receive countless tree seeds.

To bury a nut, a squirrel descends the tree carrying the seed and moves several meters out onto the forest floor. Holding the nut firmly in its teeth, the squirrel scrapes back the ground litter. Then, balancing on widespread hindlegs with tail pointed straight up, it excavates a small amount of dirt with its forepaws.

Pressing the nut into the depression, the squirrel twists it from side to side as if screwing it into the ground. Then, front incisors pound it into its final resting position. A few passes of the forefeet cover the nut with dirt and litter and the mound is solidly stamped into place. If the ground is very hard, making digging difficult, or if the litter is very thin, the cached nut may protrude in plain sight above the surface. But the squirrel considers the nut buried and does not bother with it further.

Southern flying squirrels also store a few nuts in tree branches or crotches. Although it is difficult to see them do this in the dark of night, the process is distinctly audible. Finding a suitable crevice, the squirrel twists and presses the nut firmly into place. Should it not fit, three or four more attempts are made, in good faith, before the squirrel gives up to find a new spot. Once the nut has been seated, it receives several sharp raps from front incisors. These raps can be heard for a considerable distance and I've wondered why the teeth are not damaged in the process. A few pats with forepaws make for a job well done.

When Illar Muul studied hoarding behavior in southern flying squirrels he certainly chose a species with prodigious capacity. One pair of his caged animals carried off as many as 400 nuts in a few hours. Extrapolating from his observations, Muul estimated that in a good season, under ideal weather conditions, a squirrel would be able to store as many as 15,000 nuts in a season. Whether or not such a huge number is ever stored in the wild depends on the weather, availability of nuts, and how far the squirrels have to carry the nuts for proper storage. Most small woodlots quite likely do not produce sufficient fruit to allow the squirrels to fulfill their hypothetical potential.

Keeping caged squirrels supplied with nuts for his experiments was a constant problem for Muul. To match their insatiable hoarding instinct, he removed nuts that the squirrels stored and reused them. However, it soon became apparent that the squirrels preferentially selected nuts that had not been stored before, by a margin of almost four to one, indicating that they could distinguish between the two types. Washed in detergent and rinsed, the stored nuts became more acceptable to the squirrels, suggesting that the inhibitory factor was based on smell.

Muul placed squirrels in special cages from which they could reach nuts with their forepaws but could not touch their mouths to the enticing food. From this, Muul discerned the source of the scent was from the animals' mouths. Enlarged sweat and oil glands previously had been noted in the lips of southern flying squirrels, but at the time their function was unknown. Quite likely, these glands emit the scent that labels stored nuts. Muul suggested that this scent marking enables a squirrel to identify nuts it has already stored or handled, thus it avoids processing the same nut twice.

These glands are probably also useful in marking the animal's home range, proclaiming its presence in a particular area. Constantly investigating its domain, a squirrel uses its teeth to scrape, probe, and gnaw. Sometimes it also rubs the sides of its face along branches. In this way it may be leaving its scent mark. Drops of urine also are deposited along tree branches, perhaps for the same reason.

At mealtime, southern flying squirrels again have an efficient, distinctive method for dealing with hickory nuts or pecans. Sitting on its haunches, the squirrel holds the nut in its forefeet, lower incisors rasping away at the end of the nut where the tough fruit shell is thinnest. Once the nutmeat has been exposed, the squirrel's long, slender lower incisors are used to scoop it out. When no more can be reached the squirrel resumes enlarging the hole, repeating the process until the contents have been entirely removed or the squirrel is satiated. If part of the nutmeat remains, the squirrel carefully stores the nut in a convenient crevice for later use.

The southern flying squirrel's eating style cannot be mistaken. An empty shell with a single, elliptical, smooth-edged opening at one end is an unmistakable sign that flying squirrels are present in a woodlot.

A good woodland sleuth knows this and can also distinguish the work of other rodent species. For example, when red squirrels open a nut they gnaw into it, then tear away small bits of shell leaving a hole with a ragged edge. White-footed mice, with their tiny incisors, make smooth-edged holes similar to a flying squirrel. However, they cannot reach very far into the nut to obtain the meat and must make two or three separate openings into the nut to empty it. The large, powerful fox and gray squirrels simply snap off fragments of the shell until the entire nut is dismantled.

Oaks are an abundant food plant in southern Michigan, much more common than hickories. However, oak trees produce large amounts of tannins, bitter-tasting phenolic compounds that have been used in the manufacture of leather and ink. The probable function of tannins in oaks is to reduce palatability and therefore offer the tree some protection against herbivores that eat leaves and fruits. In addition to lowering the taste appeal of the acorns, the tannins also inhibit protein assimilation within an animal's digestive tract. Thus the plant becomes a less desirable food source.

Researchers have speculated on how this affects squirrel populations that rely upon acorns as a winter food source. It is all very complicated and we still do not understand all the implications of the tannin content.

Even if squirrels could be kept informed of tannin research, it is doubtful they would care. Flying squirrels readily eat acorns. Admit-

A nut opened by a southern flying squirrel is distinguished by a single, smooth-edged, elliptical opening.

White-footed mice must gnaw several smooth-edged openings to reach all the meat.

tedly they do seem to prefer acorns of the white oak, which are lower in tannins, to those of the black or red oak. However, the latter usually produce a larger, more reliable crop of nuts. After squirrels have fed heavily upon acorns from red or black oaks, their urine becomes stained dark, almost black, from the tannins. Nevertheless, the squirrels seem to suffer no ill side-effects.

Acorns are not as easily carried as hickory nuts because the peduncle is absent. After removing the cap, a southern flying squirrel notches either side of the nut's point. The smooth acorn shell never provides a very satisfactory or secure purchase, and a seed may slip out of the squirrel's grip before reaching its destination. Successfully transported, it is buried in the same manner as the hickory nuts.

Hoarding behavior is not well documented for northern flying squirrels. What food items might they cache? Some have suggested they cut and store conifer cones, as do red squirrels, but recent evidence refutes this. Acorns, available in certain portions of the northern flying squirrel's range, are perhaps cached to some extent. Perhaps they store fungi, but again, there is no conclusive proof.

Northern flying squirrels do not display the specialized procedure of notching and carrying nuts seen in southern flying squirrels. A northern flying squirrel usually just opens its mouth wide and takes a firm grip around the middle of an acorn. A large one poses a problem because the animal cannot gape wide enough. After fumbling with an oversized acorn for some time, the squirrel finally manages to get an adequate but precarious grip on its tip.

Whether northern flying squirrels hoard food or not, by autumn the summer-born young are well-grown and able to fend for them-

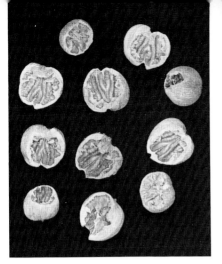
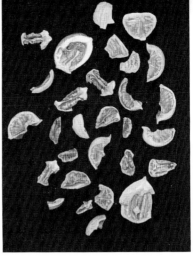

Red squirrels gnaw a rough-edged hole.

Fox squirrels and gray squirrels simply tear the nut to pieces.

selves. But I sometimes wonder about female southern flying squirrels in my woods. If a female has a late-season litter, how does lactation and caring for the family affect her ability to cache food in preparation for winter? Fortunately, in latitudes where winter is a threat, most young squirrels are reaching independence by October. However, in Michigan, families of newborn squirrels may be found as late as mid-September, requiring nurturing well into October.

I suspect the female's maternal duties take priority when the babies are very young, although she may indulge in some caching. Meanwhile, she can at least dine on the freshly ripening nuts during her nightly forays. Even if she cannot hoard as many nuts as an unencumbered animal, during winter she can search out those stored by other squirrels by using her sense of smell.

The urge to cache food occasionally overrides the squirrels' nocturnal habits and, during autumn, flying squirrels are sometimes seen during daylight hours. Intent on storing nuts, they are not deterred by the dawn, and remain out, searching for more nuts to hoard.

In the large outdoor enclosure where I keep flying squirrels for observation, the animals sometimes continue to store until ten or eleven o'clock in the morning during October and November, so long as I keep them supplied with nuts. Intensity of activity seems related to air temperature. On a cold night the squirrels restrict their movements, but if the temperature rises by early morning, the squirrels begin foraging vigorously. As if making up for lost time, they continue storing nuts several hours after sunrise.

Bird watchers have reported flying squirrels at their feeders early in the day, carrying away sunflower seeds or peanuts set out for the birds. On cloudy autumn days, hunters sometimes see flying squirrels foraging in the early morning. In fact, a bowhunter told my husband how he became the hunted during deer season. Having sat quietly in a tree stand for several hours on a cold morning, he suddenly saw a flying squirrel gliding toward him. The squirrel landed on his knee, paused a moment, then moved directly to the coat pocket containing the day's lunch. Without so much as a "by your leave" the squirrel began pulling out a sandwich. Bemused but hungry, the hunter shooed the animal away.

10. *And So To Bed*

If autumn has been generous, squirrels are well prepared for winter. Having fed heavily upon nutritious nuts, berries, seeds, and insects they are sleek and healthy with ample flesh. But this never takes the form of thick layers of fat, as it does on their relative, the woodchuck. Flying squirrels must remain agile and light; an overweight squirrel dangerously reduces its gliding efficiency.

Northern flying squirrels are, of necessity, especially well equipped to survive the harsh elements of winter in northern latitudes or high mountain elevations. Their thick, fluffy fur coats provide excellent insulation against the climate. In some regions, these squirrels grow fur on the soles of their feet in winter, partially covering the naked foot pad. Even their ears are protected by long, fine-textured hairs.

Southern flying squirrels do not possess dense, protective fur coats. Close-lying and sleek, their pelage lacks insulating loft. Feet remain sparsely furred and the thin skin of their ears is hardly protected at all. Foraging on cold winter nights, southern flying squirrels fold their ears back, nestling them as deeply as possible in the body fur to avoid frostbite.

Behavior is a primary squirrel defense against winter. Take caching, for example; a squirrel amasses a large hoard of food and then draws from it all through the cold season. Selection and preparation of a securely constructed nest is another essential behavior pattern. Snug inside its abode, the squirrel conserves vital energy reserves, which may make the difference between waiting out the final weeks of a particularly harsh winter, or succumbing before spring arrives. In addition, a squirrel in good health is more fit for the courtship season and more likely to reproduce successfully.

For the southern flying squirrels in my woodlot, the best winter home (excepting my roof) is a tree cavity with thick walls of solid wood. The squirrels add a substantial layer of nesting material, usually shredded grapevine or cedar bark. The hollow may be so crammed with bedding that one wonders how the squirrels squeeze inside. But they manage.

Large old trees with heartrot are a boon to squirrels. In the forester's terminology they are "wolf trees" and unfortunately many people think of them as worthless, something to be removed to make room for vigorous young growth. Consequently they become the target of well-meaning woodcutters. In Michigan, state and county road crews constantly search for roadside trees showing signs of rot and quickly remove them because they may possibly fall into a lane of traffic someday. These workers usually have many tales to tell of cutting trees and finding nests containing dozens of flying squirrels.

Northern flying squirrels also use tree cavities as nesting sites, but in many areas they readily construct drays of tightly woven branches or build nesting chambers inside thickly grown witches' brooms. This may be an adaptation to life in a coniferous habitat, because dead or injured conifer trees rot and collapse much more rapidly than hardwoods and thus provide fewer cavities. This is particularly true in young, second-growth conifer forests where trees are of small diameter.

In any event, after constructing its winter nest, a flying squirrel does not insist on exclusive occupancy. Nest sharing is still another behavioral accommodation for winter. During summer the largest groups are comprised of a female and her offspring, whereas most other individuals live alone or occasionally share a nest. As temperatures drop, the squirrels forsake their semi-solitary lifestyles and seek the warm comfort of a common nest. Both species of flying squirrels behave this way, but southern flying squirrels are more noted for the size of their aggregations, particularly in northern climates.

A winter aggregation of southern flying squirrels.

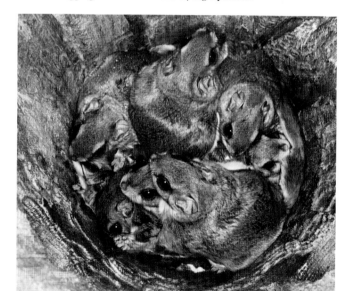

Early naturalists recognized the flying squirrel's proclivity for forming these winter aggregations. In 1743 John Brickell wrote:

> They are a tender creature, lie very warm in their nests (which are made of fine down) not appearing all the winter, being unable to bear the cold and severity of the weather, and generally half a dozen or more lie together in one nest, which is always in a hollow tree, and have there stores of provisions near them, whereon they feed during cold weather.

Brickell's observations were made in North Carolina. More recently, Alfred Avenoso of the University of Houston studied the size of aggregations in southern flying squirrel populations in Florida, comparing them to groups in more northerly portions of their range. Average winter aggregation size in Florida was 2.4 animals, while the summer mean wasn't much different at 2.0 animals. Avenoso contrasted this with Illar Muul's observations in Michigan and Massachusetts where winter aggregations averaged 5.7 squirrels and summer groups only 1.3 squirrels.

Throughout winter, the number of squirrels occupying a nest varies with weather conditions. As temperatures drop, more squirrels squeeze into the nest. During warm spells they may disperse into smaller groups until cold weather again drives them to seek a larger, communal accommodation. As might be expected, the warmth generated within a nest is a function of insulation thickness and the number of warm bodies crammed together.

The record for largest aggregation was reported by Arthur Howell in *North American Fauna;* a tree cavity in Illinois contained fifty squirrels. As many as thirteen squirrels squeezed into nestboxes during a study by Sonenshine and Levy in Virginia in January 1981. In central Arkansas, G. A. Heidt found that aggregations from September to May ranged from one to twelve squirrels, with an average of 3.9 squirrels per nest.

Within the mass of warm, furry bodies, a squirrel may curl up with feet neatly tucked underneath and tail wrapped around, quietly catching some "zzz." Or, it might sprawl outstretched, compressed in the center of the mass. Too warm, the animal squirms to the outer edge of the group; too cold, it pushes and kicks its way back to the middle, displacing another squirrel. All is fine until someone gets a foot shoved into his or her face, or other tender portion. A moment's squabble straightens things out again.

Such intimacy also allows free interchange of parasites. Should winter drag on too long the vermin population can become uncomfortable. Equally unpleasant, I should think, the animals may fail to go outside to relieve themselves of body wastes. While it has often been stated that flying squirrels fastidiously never soil their nests, I sadly report that this commendation is not always deserved. If one squirrel uses a corner of the nest as a latrine, others soon follow suit.

Several squirrel researchers have observed what seemed to be a tendency of male and female flying squirrels, of both species, to segregate into separate nests when aggregating. However, the number of nests examined in such cases was not large and I do not think the evidence is conclusive. Nests I have checked in winter were not segregated according to sex. The literature reports were from Vermont and Oregon; perhaps Michigan squirrels are more permissive and liberated.

In cold climates, southern flying squirrels remain rather inactive during winter. They do not hibernate, but forays out of the nest are kept to a minimum. If winter is too harsh, or food scarce, the squirrels will become torpid. This is not true hibernation, but a state of dormancy in which the animals reduce the rate of their body metabolism and thus conserve internal energy reserves. Illar Muul was first to report the occurrence of torpor in southern flying squirrels. Deprived of food during a period of intense cold, his research animals curled up within their boxes and their body temperatures dropped as low as 22°C (72°F), 17 degrees below normal. Intrusions into the nest did not disturb the squirrels. When lifted they remained curled up, as if unconscious. With continued handling they revived, but in some cases it required forty minutes for them to return to normal.

The severe and seemingly interminable winter of 1978 sent the southern flying squirrels in my caged colony into dormancy for more than four weeks. They even lost interest in sex. Mating was delayed by about a month. Squirrels in the wild must have responded similarly because I did not find litters of young in the woods until late April or May, four or more weeks later than usual.

At the other extreme, during an especially mild winter I kept track of southern flying squirrels inhabiting a nearby oak-hickory woodlot. Because tree cavities were scarce in the young, second-growth forest, the squirrels lived in wooden nestboxes I had erected several years previously, making it convenient for me to check on them at intervals. Throughout winter groups of two to four squirrels, male and female, crowded into the boxes, snuggling securely in nests of shredded grapevine bark.

I watched the snow cover for signs indicating squirrels were tunneling down for cached nuts, but my searching was in vain. At night I waited for the animals to exit their homes, but my efforts were unproductive. Carefully threading a four-meter ladder through the underbrush, I climbed up to the boxes to inspect them weekly during daylight hours. Each time, I found the same groups composed of the same squirrels. Not torpid, they responded to my intrusions by

A southern flying squirrel forages through frost-covered leaf litter.

squirming firmly down into the nest bottom, each trying to get under its companions. Gradually, over the weeks, the nests became more and more soiled as the animals used one corner of each box as a latrine. A few acorn shells appeared inside the boxes, from nuts brought in for consumption. Not until late February when the mating season began did the aggregations break up. Thus, it appears that even during mild winters, southern flying squirrels in my region drastically reduce their activity. Winter is a time for sleeping.

Northern flying squirrels never seem to form winter aggregations as large as those of southern flying squirrels. Perhaps this is because they are better able to withstand the rigors of winter, thus aggregating might not be as vital to their survival. On the other hand, evidence of large winter aggregations may be absent because biologists do not readily find their communal nesting sites. There are no reports of northern flying squirrels undergoing torpor.

In winter, they seem to forage more intently and over a wider area than do southern flying squirrels, either gliding from tree to tree or scampering over the snowy ground. Snowshoe-hare runways make convenient travel lanes. Pathways under fallen logs and snow-laden branches are other favored routes. Occasionally sitzmarks can be found indicating where a squirrel made a four-point landing in the snow, or a drag mark of about a half-meter shows where a squirrel made a more leisurely, gradual descent.

C. H. Merriam in *The Mammals of the Adirondack Region* wrote poetically of the northern flying squirrels' winter activity:

The Northern Flying Squirrel is a hardier animal than its smaller relative, and remains awake and active during the whole of our long and severe winters. The mercury may indicate a temperature many degrees below zero, or snow may be falling in quantities sufficient to obstruct the vision, without seeming in any way to dishearten this merry adventurer. The last rays of the departing sun have scarcely disappeared from the western horizon before the sombre shades that mark the approach of winter night commence to gather about the snowclad forest. Whether bright stars sparkle and shine through a frosty atmosphere, or heavy, leaden clouds overhang the scene, makes little difference to the Northern Flying Squirrel. He emerges from his warm nest, takes a hasty survey of the surroundings lest some wily owl should lurk hard by, glides silently to a neighboring tree, and starts forthwith upon his nightly tour in quest of food and sport.

Paul Connor of the New York State Museum gave an interesting and informative account of this species in Otsego and Schoharie counties, New York. He wrote:

. . . numerous tracks showed where these animals ran about beneath the shelter of small hemlocks and other conifers in the woods, or where the animals traveled across the snow from tree to tree . . . . Besides the tracks, the tunnels and burrows of these animals were also seen in the snow. The tracks showed where they investigated natural cavities in the snow at the base of trees and where the lower branches of the hemlocks were buried under the snow; the squirrels often enlarged these cavities by tunneling vertically downward, perhaps to search for food on the ground . . . . At this same location there was also a large log sufficiently elevated above the ground to permit the formation of a space beneath it which was banked with snow along the sides, but judging from the tracks beneath, the log was frequently traveled by flying squirrels. In several spots where the snow had drifted beneath the log, blocking the passage, the animals tunneled straight through . . . .

None were [trapped] in windy winter nights, but temperature alone does not seem to limit the activity of northern flying squirrels and they were active on the snow at temperatures at least as low as −10°F.

Northern flying squirrels may indeed be out during the coldest nights of winter, if necessary, but not because they enjoy the harsh weather. As along as it is comfortable and not unduly hungry, a squirrel remains in the nest, for nothing is to be gained by exposing itself to the elements and hungry predators. Colonies of well-fed northern flying squirrels that I maintain in southern Michigan are every bit as inactive as the nearby southern flying squirrels in a similar cage.

Both species of flying squirrels possess a carnivorous turn of appetite on occasion, but it seems to me this craving occurs most frequently in winter and early spring. Winter meals of suet or chicken heart are readily accepted by captive squirrels. When a squirrel dies in my outdoor cage during winter it is likely to be partially or wholly consumed by its former companions before I find and remove the carcass. Sometimes only the pelt remains, turned inside out and stripped clean of flesh. Squirrels dying at other seasons of the year are never mutilated in this fashion. Thus, what at first might seem predatory behavior is often merely a simple expediency for hungry squirrels during times when usual food sources are scarce.

To most people, flesh-eating squirrels seem a gruesome novelty, and probably for that reason this aspect of their ecology has frequently been commented upon in the literature. The Reverend John Bachman wrote of catching flying squirrels in box traps baited with dead blue jays, and of how the bait was often consumed by the captive squirrels.

Biologist Bernard Bailey shot a flying squirrel that emerged from a purple martin nest and found its stomach full of meat and feathers. Flying squirrels have even been noted to kill and eat mice. Curiously, only the back of the head is usually consumed and the rest of the carcass is discarded.

Once, after carefully preparing a downy woodpecker specimen, I left it out to dry overnight. That evening our resident flying squirrel discovered the study skin, carried it off behind a bookcase, and ate part of the bird's head. Fortunately, I lost only a bird specimen. In a 1911 account by B. W. Evermann and H. W. Clark, a drawer containing birdskins was left open one night and a pet flying squirrel fed on one of the skins, dying as a result of arsenic poisoning. Arsenic was often was used in the past as a specimen preservative.

Tree buds can provide winter food, and squirrels of both species snip a few. However, buds do not become really attractive until temperatures begin to rise and the buds swell in preparation for the spring flush. Oak and maple buds are avidly consumed by the squirrels in my woods, particularly the flower buds as they begin to open. Small twigs bearing flowers and leaf buds can be found in the wooden nestboxes in my woods, left there by southern flying squirrels that nibbled at the fresh, green portions. When the buds are in this attractive stage of development the squirrels will feed heavily, but this usually does not occur until April, long after the worst of winter is past.

Sap begins to flow in maple trees during late February and the squirrels gnaw away the bark to obtain the sweet fluid. Sapsucker holes provide additional access to the sap, and northern flying squirrels have been known to chew out the bark between these punctures to increase the flow. The large maple at the far end of my woodlot bears stains where sap has exuded, year after year, and scars show where squirrels annually tear away bits of bark to initiate the process.

The slight warming trend that starts maple sap flowing also brings hordes of small moths out of winter dormancy, even if snow still

The long, dark streaks on this maple's trunk resulted from squirrels gnawing its bark in late February to start the sap flowing.

lies on the ground. They, too, find the sweet sap attractive and rest on tree trunks to sip it. Flying squirrels eat some of these insects, at times engaging in spirited leaps and jumps to capture the big ones. They are an excellent source of nutrients, but two or three a night seem to be plenty. I suspect the countless, indigestible wing scales and body hairs greatly reduce their palatability.

Although the squirrels seek out any of these, and other, food sources in winter, there is no doubt that southern flying squirrels in my woodlot rely heavily upon their nut stores to carry them through to spring. An ample acorn or hickory nut crop is a good omen. Feasting on it, the squirrels come into winter well prepared; caching it, they possess a vital defense against the stinging cold.

A nut in its shell is a neat, pre-packaged winter meal. The squirrel can carry it from its caching spot to a sheltered tree cavity and eat it in relative comfort and safety. Hickory nuts are probably a more efficient winter food than acorns, being lower in tannins and thus more effectively digested. However, acorns are readily accepted if hickory nuts are not available. In any event, once a squirrel has eaten a full meal of nut meat, it can retire to its nest and sleep for a long time. In this way, it minimizes activity time and reduces its exposure to predators and unfavorable weather.

No wonder winter is the least productive season for squirrel watching. Occasionally I can entice them to the feeding station, but usually they prefer to remain curled up asleep for long periods, making only sporadic visits.

The only respite from the monotony of winter comes with the mating season. Almost overnight the squirrels forsake their conservative regimen. Peaceful coexistence no longer reigns in the aggregations; much fussing and scolding emanates from the nests. Males travel far and wide seeking females and vying for the opportunity to mate with them.

Thus, the flying squirrel's year comes full circle. Courting lasts only about two weeks. Then the aggregations quiet down, patiently enduring the last few weeks of winter, waiting for spring. By early summer a new generation of flying squirrels will be discovering the best gliding routes through the nighttime forest.

Hickory nuts remain a squirrel's favorite food throughout winter. Note the unusual white tip on this southern flying squirrel's tail.

11. *First, Catch Your Squirrel*

Flying squirrels present special problems for those wishing to study their behavior and ecology. They are small, tree-dwelling, and nocturnal. By comparison, humans are large, earth-bound creatures of the daytime, with relatively poor night vision. As I know from long experience, many hours can be spent in the woods after dark without so much as glimpsing a squirrel.

Observing them is easier when the squirrels come to us and what better way to attract them than to appeal to their stomachs? Feeding stations are an excellent means of attracting flying squirrels, luring them to a spot where they can be watched in comfort. Sometimes erecting a new feeder is not necessary because squirrels are already dining at an existing birdfeeder. But who thinks to watch a birdfeeder at night?

Having seen feeding stations attract flying squirrels on so many occasions, I wholeheartedly encourage people to try this method. Little expense is involved; a board nailed to a tree is sufficient, but the food can just as easily be placed on the ground at the tree's base. Sunflower seeds, cracked nuts, and peanut butter are probably the most alluring and effective baits. Once accustomed to using a feeder, the squirrels will tolerate illumination from a flashlight, or yard light.

A feeder placed in a suitable habitat occupied by squirrels is almost invariably discovered within a few nights and the squirrels will reveal their presence. Untouched bait, night after night, means flying squirrels do not frequent the area and the feeding station should be moved.

The efficacy of feeders varies depending on the season of the year. Squirrels are most likely to be attracted during periods of food scarcity or reproductive stress, such as early spring when females are nursing young. However, even when natural foods are plentiful, the odor of new, unfamiliar victuals sometimes seems irresistible, and squirrels will investigate if only for the sake of curiosity.

Which species will be found at the feeder will depend, of course, on geography and habitat type. In any case, when checking for squirrels at a new feeding station, one must take into consideration the different characters of the two species. Southern flying squirrels are usually quite vocal, chirping or scolding from the safety of a high tree perch when a human observer comes to inspect the feeder. Northern flying squirrels are more reticent. When a human approaches

Some squirrels take their food up to a safer height before consuming it. (SFS)

they are likely to retire and watch quietly. Therefore, if food is missing from the feeder but no squirrels are seen, scanning the nearby trees with the beam of a flashlight may be necessary. Perhaps only mice are pilfering food, but if northern flying squirrels are visiting the feeder, their bright, glowing, reddish-orange eye reflection will betray their presence. Once accustomed to using a feeder, northern flying squirrels become more bold and can be observed as they feed.

After squirrels learn the location of a feeding station, they will likely make it a prime stop on their foraging route every night, providing hours of enjoyable watching. Unfortunately, one flying squirrel looks pretty much like another, so at first it can be difficult to distinguish individual animals. But after a while, it becomes evident that although they look alike, there is great variation in their behavior and mannerisms. Often it becomes possible to recognize individuals by their actions alone. The observer can then begin to learn how the various animals interact, based on their sex, age, or social status.

When biologists study the behavior and ecology of flying squirrels in the wild, they must capture the animals to take measurements and mark them for individual identification. A feeding station isn't quite enough; live-traps are used.

This female southern flying squirrel is undisputed "boss" of my feeding station.

Baited with an attractive food, the traps are placed where the squirrels are likely to encounter them. From a review of the literature, it seems mammalogists are limited only by their imagination when concocting baits. Among those recorded as successful are dried prunes, bread, nuts, grain, sausage, bacon and bacon grease, biscuits, apples, peanut butter, dry roasted peanuts, hamburger, a dead mouse, Feensten mink bait, and fresh, dried, or decomposing flesh of mammals, birds, or fish. One wonders if hunger or merely astonishment drew the squirrels to some of these. Sunflower seeds, peanut butter, or cracked nuts are usually adequate.

Squirrels can be caught in large numbers during periods of food scarcity. One warm, rainy March evening I trapped eleven squirrels from a small woodlot in only a few hours. At other times, such as midsummer, they may completely ignore the traps for weeks at a time. Some authors have suggested flying squirrel traps be set up in the trees to facilitate capture, but such a procedure is time consuming and, in my experience, not really necessary. A promising location, patience, and luck are the main ingredients for successful trapping. Of course, a hungry squirrel helps.

Confined to a trap, a flying squirrel becomes highly vulnerable to stress through exposure. Nesting material should be supplied inside the trap to insulate the animal somewhat, but even with this precaution, leaving the trap set out overnight is risky. A squirrel entering early in the evening and remaining in the trap for many hours will quite likely be dead by morning if the air is chilled. This is particularly true for the small southern flying squirrel.

Once captured, a squirrel can be handled with thick leather gloves. However, some people are very adept at holding them firmly in their bare hands. I am not so skillful and find that an animal's loose skin enables it to squirm and wriggle, sometimes out of my grip. I prefer to transfer the squirrel to a cloth bag or insect net for greater security. Once inside, the animal can be weighed and manipulated as necessary without danger of escape.

When asked, "Don't the squirrels bite when handled?" my answer is necessarily equivocal. Flying squirrels are unusually gentle for wild animals. I often reach into nestboxes to rub a wild squirrel on the back, and it sometimes even rotates its head sideways to allow me to scratch the chin also. They vary greatly in their propensity to bite, which explains the divergent opinions held by various authors. In *Lives of Game Animals* Ernest T. Seton wrote, "The gentlest of all rodents . . . Assapan, the flyer, will rarely bite or scratch; and quickly ceases to struggle if assured that you mean to do him no grievous harm."

Zoologist H. T. Jackson remarked:

Usually one disturbed in its nest or captured in the wild will make no attempt to bite if it is gently handled, and particularly if its captor talks low or hums to it. Sometimes it may be more pugnacious, or frightened, if handled too roughly, or held too tightly, and then it will bite.

However, while studying mammals in Florida, A. L. Rand and P. Host acquired a different opinion, " . . . it is sometimes said these

A bewildered northern flying squirrel in a live trap ponders its predicament.

The notches cut in this southern flying squirrel's tail make for easy identification.

are gentle animals, reluctant to bite, but those we handled struggled and bit savagely."

In my experience, few flying squirrels bite during their initial captures, even though frightened. Nevertheless, after being handled several times, their fear is replaced by irritation and they struggle vigorously to defend themselves when held. Every squirrel is different; a few bite viciously from the very first encounter, some remain docile indefinitely. Ironic though it may seem, I generally prefer holding a naïve, wild squirrel rather than one that previously has been handled; there is less chance of being bitten.

Of course, I try not to allow squirrels to bite me, but avoiding their lightning-fast defense can be difficult. The best protection against flying squirrel teeth is a pair of insulated ski gloves; the padding in the insulation prevents teeth from reaching fingers. Ordinary cowhide is ineffective. Razor-sharp incisors slice through the toughest leather, penetrating to the fingers beneath.

Squirrels can be marked for individual identification. For short-term projects, tufts of fur can be snipped out of the squirrel's flattened tail in a distinctive, predetermined pattern. This is easily done. The tail molts only once a year; thus depending on when the clipping is done, such marking can be useful for up to ten or eleven months. Tail marks of this nature can be seen from some distance away. For someone watching a group of squirrels at a bird feeder outside the living room window, tail marks make it possible to keep track of who's who.

Ear tags are usually more enduring as identification markers for long-term projects. One of these numbered strips of metal is clamped onto a squirrel's ear, causing minimal discomfort. Tags may last indefinitely, although they occasionally rip out of the thin skin of the squirrel's ear. Jacalyn Madden reported in her studies that about 30 percent of the squirrels lost their tags over time. I have tagged northern flying squirrels that retained the marker for several years.

Once the squirrels have been marked for identification, they can be trapped repeatedly over their home range to gain some idea of where they roam and how long they live. It is a slow, laborious method for gathering information; a lot of movements are missed. Countless questions are left unanswered.

Because of these problems, and the difficulties of observing the squirrels directly, as one might watch a fox or gray squirrel, few in-depth studies of wild flying squirrels were conducted in the past. However, in recent years, several highly successful studies of flying squirrels have been done with the aid of radio transmitters. Weighing only a few grams, these enable a researcher to follow the movements of an individual animal without ever seeing it. With the help of such modern technology, flying squirrel research is now more efficient and informative, although probably no less laborious.

Granted, there are problems. As might be expected, the squirrels object to wearing neck collars. Jacalyn Madden can attest that southern flying squirrels are particularly bad offenders in this respect. In her studies, nestmates of a squirrel wearing a collar often chewed and destroyed the expensive radio transmitter the very first night it was worn. It was enough to break a biologist's heart, and pocketbook. Madden was able to alleviate this problem somewhat by encasing the unit in epoxy containing red cayenne pepper, but some squirrels seemed to develop a taste for the pepper. Aluminum polishing grit was more repugnant to the squirrels and finally Madden was able to get a full fifty days use from a collar before the battery expired.

Jacalyn Madden monitors a southern flying squirrel's movements with radiotelemetry gear.

Northern flying squirrels seem more amenable to high-tech research. Robert Mowrey in Alaska assured me he maintained collars on squirrels for three months or more. On one occasion a squirrel retained its collar for six months, long after the battery expired. Both squirrel and transmitter were in fine shape when the animal eventually was recaptured.

Mowrey used a team of four assistants in his radiotracking work. Stationed near a squirrel's daytime retreat at dusk they followed the animal through the dark forest as it foraged, staying with it until it retired at the end of its activity period. In this way they were able to map foraging routes, feeding locations, and den sites. How else could such information be obtained?

I have never been so ambitious in my flying squirrel studies. My favorite method of monitoring flying squirrel populations is to use nestboxes. These work best where natural cavities are scarce, such as in a young woodlot. Under such circumstances, wild squirrels readily accept artificial structures. In southern Michigan, young oak forests are an ideal site for nestboxes to attract southern flying squirrels; food is present, but nesting sites are lacking. In the Upper Peninsula I have known northern flying squirrels to frequent nestboxes in jack pine forests where tree cavities were scarce.

Supplying boxes in such habitats may very well result in an increase in the squirrel population, and one has to keep this in mind when interpreting the data collected. Nevertheless, nestboxes are an excellent tool because the squirrels are easily accessible.

A nestbox constructed of lumber.

A nestbox constructed from a section of hollow log.

Nestboxes are appealing because, unlike radio collars, anyone can construct and use them. My boxes are built of lumber that is 2.5 centimeters (1 inch) thick, and have inside dimensions of 13 by 13 by 31 centimeters (5 by 5 by 12 inches), with an entrance hole of 3 centimeters (1¼ inch) for southern flying squirrels or 4 centimeters (1½ inch) for northern flying squirrels.

The entrance to this fine home is near to the tree trunk when the box is set out. I like to add a "porch," a board or stick beneath the entrance, to provide a better grip for the squirrels. The front wall of the box can be opened outward because it is attached with a hinge at the bottom and a hook near the top. Thus the box can easily be opened to check for squirrels or for its semiannual cleaning.

It does not seem to matter to which side of the tree the box is attached, but our prevailing winds are from the west so I turn the entrance hole to the east. Putting nails into a tree to attach the nestbox is often not a good idea; even the thought of it is enough to make a forester cry. The nestbox will rot eventually, but the steel nails will remain. The tree will grow around them, concealing the foreign objects within its wood. When the tree is cut up for firewood or lumber the nails will have a ruinous impact on saw teeth. Unfortunately, nails are undeniably the easiest and most efficient method for attaching the nestbox. Such a dilemma.

I try to compromise. When putting up a box I avoid fine, straight trees that may one day make excellent lumber. I look for deformed, misshapen trees, or trees of species that have little timber value. I also use aluminum nails instead of steel; the softer metal does less damage to cutting edges.

Where human disturbance is a problem, I use a ladder to attach boxes out of reach. Squirrels prefer to have their pre-fab homes placed as high as possible, but if vandalism is not a consideration I place them at a height of 2 meters (6 feet) where they can be checked without maneuvering a long ladder through the underbrush.

Often squirrels find the boxes within a matter of days and move into their new homes. Red squirrels, mice, and yellow jackets may usurp some of the houses, and after mammals have built their nests, bumblebees sometimes burrow into the nesting material. When angry buzzing emanates from a box I am about to open, I give it a wide berth.

To check inside a box, I open the front and peer in. Finding a flying squirrel at home, I encircle the entrance hole with a net and gently tap on the box, inducing the squirrel to leap out into the net. After a few such experiences, however, a squirrel learns my routine and refuses to leave the box, cowering down in the nesting material instead. Then it must be encouraged with a gentle nudge. If this fails,

It takes experience to learn how to hold a wriggling flying squirrel. (SFS)

I cover the animal with the net and lift it out. When several squirrels are sharing a box, they push and shove under each other, each striving to be at the bottom of the heap to avoid capture. Even a mother with young of weaning age will ungallantly resort to this ploy, attempting to hide beneath her offspring.

By checking on the squirrels at weekly intervals, or even more often, I can keep records of their reproductive cycles, weight changes, molting periods, litter sizes, and similar parameters. I admit I am biased, but flying squirrels are fun to study. Never do I tire of admiring their handsome good looks and pert behavior. Sometimes I feel rather like a grandmother as I watch yet another generation of young squirrels grow to maturity in one of the homes I provided.

Although serious studies of flying squirrels may seem to be the domain of trained scientists with expensive equipment such as radiotracking gear, anyone living in flying squirrel country can have the pleasure of associating with these delightful animals. If they seem rare, it is only because we have failed to make the effort to meet them. Fortunately, this is easily rectified. All it takes is a small offering of food and shelter.

12. *Assapan*

A small beast they have they call Assapanick, but we call them flying squirrels, because spreading their legs, and so stretching the largeness of their skins, that they have beene seene to fly 30 to 40 yards.

So wrote Captain John Smith, Governor of the Jamestown Colony in 1606. It is the first written reference to the North American flying squirrel.

Smith's account apparently sparked the imagination of King James I, because in 1609 the Earl of Southampton, council member of the Virginia Company, wrote to the Earl of Salisbury, the King's Secretary of State:

Talkinge with the King by chance I tould him of the Virginia squirills which they say will fly . . . and hee presently and very earnestly asked me if none of them was provided for him and whether your Lordship had none for him, sayinge that hee was sure you would gett him one of them. I would not have troubled you with this but that you know so well how hee is affected to these toyes. . . .

Unfortunately, I have been unable to learn the results of this delightful exchange and if the King did, indeed, acquire any flying squirrels.

Because of their confiding nature and unusual gliding ability, flying squirrels have been kept as pets for centuries. King James may have made a royal request for a flying squirrel, but the colonists enjoyed keeping them, too. In 1770 John Kalm wrote:

Among all the squirrels in this country, [flying squirrels] are the most easily tamed. The boys carry them to school, or wherever they go, without their ever attempting to escape; if even they put their squirrel aside, it leaps upon them again immediately, creeps either into their bosom, or their sleeve, or any fold of the clothes, and lies down to sleep.

F. H. King described his pets in 1883:

I have never known wild animals that became so perfectly familiar and confiding as these young squirrels did; and they seemed to get far more enjoyment from playing upon my person than in any other place, running in and out of pockets, and between my coat and vest. After the frolic was over they always esteemed it a great favor if I would allow them to crawl into my vest in front and go to sleep there, where they felt the warmth of my body. . . . If they

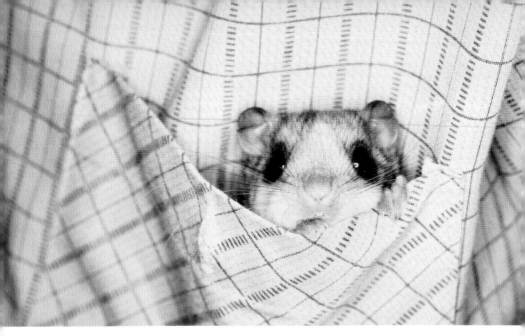

A young northern flying squirrel discovers that clothes provide a convenient retreat.

escaped from the cage during the night, I was sure to be warned of the fact by their coming into the bed to roll themselves up close to my face or neck.

Even today, flying squirrels continue to be popular as pets. Animal dealers often include flying squirrels in their inventory. Flying squirrels are protected species in several states and a special permit is required before squirrels can be obtained.

Either as pets or as lab animals, flying squirrels are not difficult to maintain in good health in captivity as long as a few precautions are taken in their diet. If allowed to do so, some squirrels will dine almost exclusively on nuts and sunflower seeds. These are an excellent food

A southern flying squirrel samples some of the native fare.

source for the most part, but tend to be deficient in calcium and vitamin D. Consequently, the squirrels are prone to suffer osteomalacia, a disease characterized by deformed, unmineralized bone, cataracts, and loss of hair. If the deficiency is not corrected, the animals often die or suffer permanent deformation. Therefore, care must be taken to see that they eat a variety of foods, especially those containing calcium and vitamin D, for example, milk products, shelled corn, and bananas.

As house pets, flying squirrels are lively and entertaining, but not without drawbacks. For one thing, they cannot be house-trained. Allowed free run, they leave small, mouselike droppings everywhere as well as occasional puddles on tables or wet spots on furniture and curtains. Being rodents, they also have a strong urge to gnaw on things and small toothmarks soon appear on woodwork, furniture, books, and other household objects.

A southern flying squirrel in search of a nest site.

Private, quiet—this will make a fine nest site. (SFS)

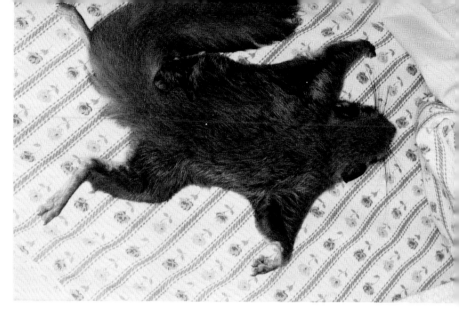

A northern flying squirrel stretches out for a nap on soft, clean sheets.

When young, flying squirrels are uncontainably active and playful. Quite willing to associate with humans, they run about on people, ducking inside shirts and blouses for security. Visitors do not always appreciate this and I have seen guests almost climb out of their clothes after a squirrel slipped inside. Fast and agile, the squirrels are nearly impossible to stop. As zoologist Ernest P. Walker commented, "Some of my friends suddenly develop remarkable agility when the squirrels get inside their clothes. To the squirrels it is almost as good as scampering about in a hollow tree!"

At six to nine months of age, squirrels become very independent and often do not appreciate being handled. Although tame and willing to climb about on a person and be stroked, they object to being confined in any manner. Handled against their wishes, they scold and sometimes even bite. A person keeping squirrels as pets must accept that flying squirrels are not domesticated. They are tame but still wild animals, and their instincts for self-preservation must be respected.

Allowed the run of a house, a mature squirrel will build a nest in a place of its own choosing; interacting with humans loses priority. Tissues, lint, handkerchiefs, or other small scraps of material are carried off and incorporated into the nest. The squirrel can become very insistent upon having its way, as in the case of a pregnant female squirrel that nested in our linen closet. When we came near she aggressively attacked and bit, although under other circumstances she was perfectly well-mannered.

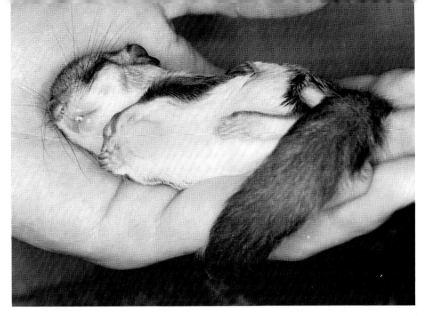

After a romp, a young flying squirrel can fall asleep just about anywhere. (SFS)

Young flying squirrels can be encouraged into activity at almost any time of the day or night. However, mature squirrels become increasingly nocturnal and resent being disturbed from their sleep. Eventually, human and squirrel schedules barely overlap. The squirrels are active for two to four hours in the evening and again for a few hours before sunrise.

In spite of these drawbacks, squirrel owners sometimes become very attached to their pets, even taking them traveling. One devoted squirrel owner claimed his was the first flying squirrel to have passed through the Holland Tunnel, flown in an airplane over Cincinnati, peered from the top of the Washington Monument, visited the Wright Memorial at Kitty Hawk, and sailed around Bonaventure Island. It covered a total of 24,000 kilometers (15,000 miles) in its lifetime.

This southern flying squirrel didn't think much of the cocktail, but the cherry was delicious, thank you.

Illustration by Anthony Taber. *Reproduced courtesy of the artist.*

People with young flying squirrels in captivity sometimes worry that their wards will not learn to glide and so attempt to give the animals lessons. Usually these consist of gently tossing the squirrel toward a suitable landing site such as a hanging blanket or convenient stump. One surrogate mother gradually lengthened the toss until he was throwing the squirrels for a distance of 15 meters (50 feet) or more. If he threw the animals into the air away from the stump, they would turn and glide back in the correct direction. Other people simply toss the squirrel into the air and allow it to glide back to them like an animated boomerang.

After hearing such tales, I tried tossing flying squirrels. Some animals seem to enjoy it; others never appreciate the experience. The best method is a slow, underhand swing. If the squirrel is willing to become a projectile it will assist by giving a strong kick with its hindfeet at the moment it leaves my hand. At other times the squirrel curls up on its back in my hand and allows itself to become airborne by my efforts alone. A squirrel not wishing to be thrown grips with claws and hangs on.

Gliding lessons are not necessary, but if the animals are started when young they seem to enjoy the sport. Wrote Laura Heinold:

Two country boys who were childhood playmates of mine enjoyed the most unique game of catch I've ever known. They would toss back and forth a bright-eyed little animal in cinnamon fur. Probably the first of the guided missiles, their "ball" was a pet flying squirrel.

The games's fascination was enhanced by the flying squirrel's willing participation. He would squeek and twitter to attract attention when the boys walked past his cage. No matter how hard he was thrown, the squirrel was always in control of himself. Checking his momentum in mid-air, he would land in the catcher's hands with a helicopter's timing. If the throw happened to be wild, the squirrel automatically corrected it by banking and steering unerringly to his destination.

13. *The Quaintest Little Sprite*

Mogens Nielsen, a friend employed by the Michigan Department of Natural Resources, is a leading authority on Michigan butterflies and moths although their study is only his avocation. One night, in an isolated area of northern Michigan, "Mo" was pursuing his hobby of collecting moths by attracting them with fermented bait to tree trunks. Just as he was reaching for a particularly attractive moth tippling at the bait, an unexpected slap on the back caused him to freeze in his tracks. Mo had thought himself miles from the nearest human company.

With heart pounding, he turned to face the intruder only to find himself eye-to-eye with a large flying squirrel resting on his shoulder. The squirrel reacted first, leaping to the tree and snatching up the moth. Quickly scampering up the tree, the thief launched itself into the night and was gone.

Flying squirrels normally have few unpleasant encounters with humans and consequently have not learned to be as wary of us as are other squirrel species. It is often surprising to discover, as Mo did, just how bold these animals can be when in their element. No longer are they the sleepy, lethargic creatures we observe during daylight hours when we disturb them from their nests.

I still recall my first, fleeting acquaintance with a flying squirrel. As a youngster camping under the sky, I lay sleeplessly watching patterns the fire cast on surrounding trees, when suddenly a flash of white caught my eye. In an instant, a southern flying squirrel landed on a tree trunk, only a few meters above my head. Bright-eyed and alert, the animal silently inspected the strange apparition of a dozen humans, lying scattered on the forest floor in cloth cocoons. Imagine its impression of humans—such sleepy, lethargic creatures. Then, as suddenly as it appeared, the squirrel bounded up the tree and disappeared into the night.

Other campers sleeping under the stars have reported their own close encounters with flying squirrels. One man wrote of squirrels "crossing and recrossing my bed which was situated under a large, red fir tree." At other times, tiny pieces of bark may shower down on someone reposing under a busy flying squirrel tree.

Even tent-campers have their brushes with flying squirrels. Mammalogist Vasco M. Tanner described an episode at Mount Timpanogos, Utah:

These little night prowlers are fond of cultivated cherries and would come into the tents for them. Some of the squirrels chose as their midnight sport that of "shooting the shoot" by sliding down the tents.

Bouncing on tent roofs seems to be a standard flying squirrel antic. Similar reports come from the Okefenokee Swamp of Georgia, and Yosemite Park in California. At the latter location, an assistant naturalist remarked that he received complaints from campers that the squirrels repeatedly slid and ran down the roofs of tents as the occupants tried to sleep. A tent roof apparently makes a soft landing site, like a trampoline perhaps.

Ernest T. Seton told an amusing story of flying squirrel transgression in *Lives of Game Animals:*

An odd experience befell Mr. Hunter during his return from a hunting trip to the settlement last fall. One evening he left a candle burning on the table in the Forty-Nine-Mile Camp while he went out to the hovel to look after the horses. To his surprise, when he returned to the camp the candle was not only extinguished, but could nowhere be found! Mr. Hunter is not entirely free from the influence of these wild, weird legends peculiar to the backwoods of the Miramichi, especially those that relate to a fabulous monster known as the "Dungarvon Hooper." He lit another candle, however, and went out to attend to his team. When he came back he found that the second candle had vanished as mysteriously as the first! This was a severe blow to Mr. Hunter's peace of mind, but he pulled himself together and examined the camp thoroughly to see if some practical joker was not concealed about the premises. Finding no traces of anything in human form, he placed this third and last candle on the table, stood his axe within easy reach, and awaited developments. In a few minutes a flying-squirrel hopped in the door, boldly mounted the table and knocked down the candle, thus extinguishing the flame. He started for the door with his booty when Mr. Hunter took a hand and put the little rascal to flight.

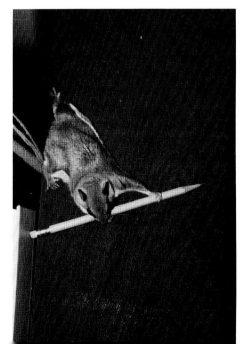

Pet squirrels sometimes have an irritating propensity for carrying off small objects.

That was not the only house haunted by flying squirrels. Vernon Bailey wrote about another in *The Mammals and Life Zones of Oregon:*

> In a log cabin back in the mountains where some old settlers resided, an old-fashioned spinning wheel was long stored in the attic. This wheel was sometimes heard revolving at night when no one was near it and was often found still in motion when examined. The house finally acquired the reputation of being haunted until one brave member of the family stole silently up to the dark room when the whirring of the wheel was heard and with a flashlight saw [a flying squirrel] running on top of the wheel as it spun beneath the animal's skillful tread.

If they do no damage, flying squirrels are often welcome nighttime visitors in human habitations. C. B. Moore commented in *The Book of Wild Pets:*

> As boys, we lived on the edge of the campus of Mt. Holyoke College, South Hadley, Mass. It was a common occurrence for flyers to sail into our open bedroom window and right onto our bed in the evening from a nearby tree whose limbs touched the side of the house. We handled and fed them on nuts and fruits.

Nevertheless, whenever wild animals live in close association with humans, problems are bound to occur. How do flying squirrels rate as pests?

Fortunately, in this role they have little stature. As mentioned, they can become nuisances if they take up residence in a house. Besides making noise at night with their uninhibited activity, the squirrels may cause damage by getting into boxes of stored clothes, paper, or other material that offers the makings of a comfortable nest. Of course, if too numerous inside a house, they can pose a health hazard because of their parasites.

In a short note in the 1926 *Journal of Mammalogy*, F. M. Fryxell described several populations of prolific and bothersome urban flying squirrels. He wrote:

> It has become necessary in several cities of the Middle West to wage war on flying squirrels, for in recent years, they have grown so numerous and troublesome as to constitute a civic nuisance . . . . One mystified resident from Davenport [Iowa] brought a couple of flying squirrels to the writer and desired to know the name of the "funny rats" that had invaded the premises and neighborhood, and that were constantly being brought in by his cat. . . . The small, active rodents gain access through windows, crevices under the eaves, and similar apertures to the attics of homes, and here, according to the complainers, they make considerable noise at night.

Situations like this occur only occasionally, when squirrel populations peak.

Caught in the act. (SFS)

In the early settlement days of our country, flying squirrels were sometimes implicated as agricultural pests because they reportedly consumed corn planted in the homesteaders' small clearings in the forest. Perhaps they were pests to some degree, but their depredations were undoubtedly minor compared to those of the fox and gray squirrels, and other wildlife species.

To the best of my knowledge, today they are considered agricultural pests only in pecan orchards. Pecans are probably the most highly prized of all nuts by the southern flying squirrel in the southeastern United States. Occasionally the squirrels' feeding can be excessive if they are too abundant, but again, their nocturnal depredations usually go undetected, or are blamed on the gray squirrels visible in the orchards during the day.

Bird-lovers sometimes consider flying squirrels pests because they have a reputation, not always deserved, for killing birds and stealing eggs. They also may compete with cavity nesters for home sites. People who put out bluebird houses sometimes claim to find up to 100 percent occupancy by southern flying squirrels with clear destruction of eggs. Yet birds and squirrels can coexist. George H. Lowrey, Jr., author of *The Mammals of Louisiana and its Adjacent Waters*, reported a purple martin house where six flying squirrels lived along with a number of birds.

A playful northern flying squirrel juvenile, momentarily restrained.

Squirrels of all sorts are the bane of the backyard birdfeeder. The Audubon Society is constantly beset with pleas from people desperate for methods of keeping fox and gray squirrels out of their expensive sunflower seeds. Flying squirrels are not normally considered nuisances, probably only because few people realize they are out there, industriously working the night shift.

Keeping flying squirrels out of a feeder can be as difficult and disheartening as ostracizing the diurnal squirrels, because the gliders are equally persistent. George H. Harrison, author of *The Backyard Birdwatcher*, told of a family that watched one evening as a flying squirrel made forty-six attempts to land on a bird feeder before finally hitting it just right. Thereafter it never again erred and subsequently enjoyed bountiful rations. They noted with rueful admiration that the squirrel could consume ten seeds a minute, sometimes for as long as twenty-five minutes without stopping.

Epilogue

Ending is difficult. There remain so many more fragments of squirrel lore to discuss, so many more questions to ponder, so many more tales to relate. Even the minor scraps help convey an impression of their mannerisms and behavior. But sadly, as my editor discreetly advised, this is not an encyclopedia; it is not intended to contain every conceivable bit of information on flying squirrels. For those readers interested in learning more, the bibliography should be a useful place to start.

Of course, the best way to learn about flying squirrels is simply to go out and enter their twilight world. They are quite willing to share it. I hope I have encouraged at least a few people to do so. Perhaps the most vivid lesson to be learned is that each squirrel is an individual, slightly different from the others in its behavior. Even its physical appearance differs, although this is sometimes difficult for our untrained eyes to discern.

Flying squirrels of either species are endowed with certain instincts and patterns of behavior, but the expression of those traits varies widely. Squirrels are not rigidly programmed, like robots. They have the same five senses that we have and a brain. They receive signals from the world surrounding them, and respond to those signals. In each situation individuals react a little differently, but this flexibility is why they are so fascinating.

It also indicates why the study of animal behavior can seem a rather inexact science at times, although every day researchers find new ways of quantifying it. Some of us rejoice at the eternal variation inherent in animal behavior. To know that life will never be entirely predictable and dull is reassuring to me. At other times it is a bit humbling. Several knowledgeable flying squirrel researchers read and commented upon the manuscript for this book. Their most common reaction was to remark how the squirrels at their study sites behaved differently from the ones I described.

Thus, the study of flying squirrels, or indeed any living thing, is a truly unending challenge. Every day brings some new bit of knowledge or understanding, and simultaneously opens doors to still more unanswered questions. Who would wish it otherwise?

So, if you will pardon me, I shall close now. It is dusk. The flying squirrels are stirring in the woods. I must resume my squirrel-watching—a lifetime of it.

Appendix A: Literature Records of Flying Squirrel Habitats

TABLE 1

Habitats occupied by southern flying squirrels.

Location	Description
United States:	
Arkansas (Central)	Forests of oak, sweetgum, pine, black gum, red maple, and hickory (Heidt, 1977).
Florida (Northeastern)	Live oak hammocks and turkey oak stands; swamps, bayheads (Moore, 1946).
Georgia	Hardwood forests and coastal turkey oak-pine association (Golley, 1962).
Georgia, Okefenokee Swamp	Pine barrens, cypress bays, live-oak hammocks (Harper, 1927).
Illinois (Southern)	Upland forests of oak, hickory, beech, and hard maple; isolated oak-hickory woodlots; swampy woodlands of black oak, sweet gum, and red maple (Layne, 1958).
Maine (Southwestern)	Mature mixed hardwoods of predominantly red oak, sugar maple, beech, and yellow birch (Cameron, 1976).
Maryland	Cut-over cypress swamps with white cedar, red maple, and loblolly pine (Muul, 1968).
Massachusetts	Red maple, oak, and white pine association; oak-maple forests; beech-maple forests; shrub oak woodlands; stands of mixed gray birch-oak-hemlock; aspen groves with scattered oak (Muul, 1968).
Michigan	Oak-hickory forests; aspen with scattered oak (Muul, 1968).
Minnesota	Mature hardwood forests of basswood, sugar maple, elm, and oak; oak-aspen stands; forests in the "birch-pine-spruce-fir belt" (Gunderson and Beer, 1953).
New York (Eastern)	Sugar maple and beech woods with some hemlock; red oak and white oak forests; mature hemlock stands (Connor, 1960).
New York, Long Island	Forests of black oak, red maple, white oak, and hickory (Madden, 1974). Woodlands of assorted oaks or other deciduous trees; pitch pine; mixed pitch pine and oak; southern white cedar; sandy pine barrens of pitch pine and oak (Connor, 1971).
Pennsylvania	Beech-maple forests (Sollberger, 1940).

Location	Description
Virginia (Central Piedmont)	Mixed forests of predominantly white oak, red oak, yellow poplar, hickory, and sweet gum (Sonenshine and Levy, 1981).
Wisconsin	Forests of deciduous trees; old orchards; mixed hardwoods and conifers (Jackson, 1961).
Mexico:	
State of Michoacán	Pine-oak forests (Hooper, 1952).
State of Oaxaca	Dry pine and oak covered mountain slopes (Goodwin, 1961).
State of Vera Cruz	Cloud forests (Goodwin, 1961).

TABLE 2

Habitats occupied by northern flying squirrels.

Location	Description
United States:	
Alaska	Taiga forests of white spruce and paper birch interspersed with groves of quaking aspen (Dice, 1921).
California (Northeastern)	Ponderosa pine forests; lodgepole pine forests; stands of mixed red fir and white fir (McKeever, 1960).
Michigan	Sugar maple, yellow birch, and hemlock forests; jack pine barrens; white cedar swamps (Manville, 1949).
New York (Southeastern)	Forests of beech, maple sugar, red oak, various birches, and other deciduous trees with some hemlock and white pine; pure beech-maple forests; stands of red spruce, balsam fir, and hemlock (Connor, 1960).
North Carolina– Appalachian Mountains	Spruce-fir forests; mature hardwood forests of beech, yellow birch, maple, hemlock, red oak, and buckeye (Weigl, 1977).
North Carolina– Tennessee border, Appalachian Mountains	Ecotone between spruce-fir forests and hardwood forests of beech, sugar maple, buckeye, and yellow birch (Weigl and Osgood, 1974).
Pennsylvania (Northcentral)	Beech, yellow birch, and sugar maple forests (Doutt, 1930).
Wisconsin	Mature forests of mixed conifers and deciduous trees, preferably moist with fallen, mossy logs; stands of white cedar, spruce or balsam fir; hemlock-maple or hemlock-gray birch forests (Jackson, 1961).
Utah (Southwestern)	Engelmann spruce forests; streamside stands of white fir with cottonwood (Musser, 1961).
Canada:	
Alberta	Mixed woods with tall conifers, or semi-open woods (Soper, 1970).

Appendix B: Origins of North American Flying Squirrels

As small, tree-dwelling animals, North American flying squirrels are poorly represented in the fossil record. Their fragile bones were rarely deposited in situations conducive to preservation. Consequently, origins and early distribution of North American gliders remain a mystery, and zoologists engage largely in speculation when discussing their past history.

Thirty-three species of flying squirrels are presently found in Asia; presumably this region represents their center of evolution and dispersal. Ancestors of our native squirrels are thought to have migrated here in the distant past when conditions for passage were suitable. Current opinion is that ancestors of the two North American species arrived separately.

William Burt first hypothesized that our northern flying squirrel is more closely related to an Asian species of flying squirrel than it is to the southern flying squirrel, basing his theory on morphology of the baculum, a bone in the squirrel's penis. The northern flying squirrel's baculum is more similar to that of *Hylopetes*, an Asian genus, than to that of the southern flying squirrel. Burt postulated that the ancestral northern flying squirrel migrated to North America across a Bering land bridge at a much later date than did the ancestral stock for the southern flying squirrel.

Both Illar Muul and Peter Weigl subsequently elaborated on this theme. During the early Miocene, 20 to 25 million years ago, global weather conditions were milder than they are now, and a diverse Arcto-Tertiary forest covered much of the northern hemisphere, including the Bering land bridge connecting Eurasia with North America. The southern flying squirrel antecedents probably migrated through this mixed deciduous-coniferous forest, following a path across northern Canada to what is now the eastern United States, a route also followed by several other mammal species. Much later, during a favorable weather period in the Pleistocene about 100,000 years ago, southern flying squirrels migrated along a corridor of suitable habitat through Texas into Mexico and Central America, where we still find relict populations of this species.

Global weather conditions deteriorated in the late Miocene and the Arcto-Tertiary forest of the Bering land bridge was gradually replaced by a boreal forest. During the early Pliocene, 10 to 12 million years ago, a different species of Asian flying squirrel, one adapted to boreal habitat, migrated into North America. This was the ancestral stock of the northern flying squirrel. Boreal forest covered the breadth of the continent and the squirrels dispersed into a similarly broad range.

The distributions we see today, then, result from these earlier migrations. Further faunal interchanges have not occurred because the Bering land bridge is no longer extant. Although less extensive than formerly, boreal forest still covers a broad continental range and northern flying squirrels are found throughout this habitat. Southern flying squirrels reside in the favorable deciduous and deciduous-pine habitats of the eastern United States. The corridor of habitat leading to Mexico has disappeared, isolating the Mexican and Central American populations from those to the north.

Bibliography

Allen, J. A. 1877. Monographs of North American Rodentia. U.S. Geological Survey, Washington, D.C.

Audubon, J. J. and J. Bachman. 1851. The Viviparous Quadrupeds of North America. V. G. Audubon, New York, 2:1–334.

Avenoso, A. C., Jr. 1968. Selection and Processing of Nuts by the Flying Squirrel *Glaucomys volans*. Ph.D. dissertation, University of Florida.

Bailey, B. 1923. Meat-eating Propensities of Some Rodents of Minnesota. *Journal of Mammalogy* 4:129.

———. 1929. Mammals of Sherburne County, Minnesota. *Journal of Mammalogy* 10:153–164.

Bailey, V. 1936. The Mammals and Life Zones of Oregon. *North American Fauna* 55:1–416.

Baillie, J. L., Jr. 1930. Outside Nests of Flying Squirrels. *Canadian Field-Naturalist* 44:94.

Barkalow, F. S., Jr. 1956. A Handicapped Flying Squirrel, *Glaucomys volans*. *Journal of Mammalogy* 37:122–123.

Booth, E. S. 1946. Notes on the Life History of the Flying Squirrel. *Journal of Mammalogy* 27:28–30.

Brickell, J. 1743. *The Natural History of North Carolina*. Dublin, printed for the author.

Brink, C. H. and F. C. Dean. 1966. Spruce Seed as a Food of Red Squirrels and Flying Squirrels in Interior Alaska. *Journal of Wildlife Management* 30:503–512.

Burt, W. H. 1960. Bacula of North American Mammals. *Miscellaneous Publications, Museum of Zoology, The University of Michigan* 113:1–76.

Cameron, D. M., Jr. 1976. Distribution of the Southern Flying Squirrel (*Glaucomys volans*) in Maine. *Canadian Field-Naturalist* 90:173–174.

Catesby, M. 1743. The Natural History of Carolina, Florida, and the Bahama Islands. Vol. 2. London.

Connor, P. F. 1960. The Small Mammals of Otsego and Schoharie Counties, New York. New York State Museum, *Science Service Bulletin* 382:1–84.

———. 1966. The Mammals of the Tug Hill Plateau, New York. New York State Museum, *Science Service Bulletin* 406:1–82.

———. 1971. The Mammals of Long Island, New York. New York State Museum, *Science Service Bulletin* 416:1–78.

Coventry, A. F. 1932. Notes on the Mearns Flying Squirrel. *Canadian Field-Naturalist* 46:75–78.

Cowan, I. McT. 1936. Nesting Habits of the Flying Squirrel *Glaucomys sabrinus*. *Journal of Mammalogy* 17:58–60.

Cuvier, F. G. 1825. *Des Dents des Mammifères, Considérées comme Caractères Zoologiques*. F. G. Levrault. Strasbourg.

Cuvier, G. 1800. *Leçons d'Anatomie Comparée de G. Cuvier*. Vol. 1. Baudouin, Paris.

DeCoursey, P. J. 1959. Daily Activity Rhythms in the Flying Squirrel, *Glaucomys volans*. Ph.D. dissertation, University of Wisconsin.

———. 1960. Daily Light Sensitivity Rhythm in a Rodent. *Science* 131:33–35.

Dice, L. R. 1921. Notes on the Mammals of Interior Alaska. *Journal of Mammalogy* 2:20–28.

Diersing, V. E. 1980. Systematics of Flying Squirrels, *Glaucomys volans* (Linnaeus), from Mexico, Guatemala, and Honduras. *Southwestern Naturalist* 2:157–172.

Dolan, P. G. and D. C. Carter. 1977. *Glaucomys volans*. Mammalian Species 78:1–6. *American Society of Mammalogists.*

Doutt, J. K. 1930. *Glaucomys sabrinus* in Pennsylvania. *Journal of Mammalogy* 11:239–240.

Duma, R. J., et al. 1981. Epidemic Typhus in the United States Associated with Flying Squirrels. *Journal of the American Medical Association* 245:2318–2323.

Errington, P. L. 1935. Food habits of Mid-West Foxes. *Journal of Mammalogy* 16:192–200.

Evermann, B. W. and H. W. Clark. 1911. Notes on the Mammals of the Lake Maxinkuckee Region. *Proceedings of the Washington Academy of Science* 13:1–34.

Ferron, J. 1983. Scent Marking by Cheek Rubbing in the Northern Flying Squirrel *(Glaucomys sabrinus)*. *Canadian Journal of Zoology* 61:2377–2380.

Findley, J. S. 1945. The Interesting Fate of a Flying Squirrel. *Journal of Mammalogy* 26:437.

Flying Squirrels in Flight. 1949. *Life* 27(22) 16–18.

Foster, W. L. and J. Tate, Jr. 1966. The Activities and Coactions of Animals at Sapsucker Trees. *The Living Bird* 5:87–113.

Fryxell, F. M. 1926. Flying Squirrels as City Nuisances. *Journal of Mammalogy* 7:133.

Goertz, J. W., R. M. Dawson, and E. E. Mowbray. 1975. Response to Nest Boxes and Reproduction by *Glaucomys volans* in Northern Louisiana. *Journal of Mammalogy* 56:933–939.

Golley, F. B. 1962. *Mammals of Georgia*. University of Georgia Press, Athens. 218 pp.

Goodwin, G. G. 1961. Flying Squirrels *(Glaucomys volans)* of Middle America. *American Museum Novitates* 2059:1–22.

Gordon, D. C. 1962. Adirondack Record of Flying Squirrels above Timber Line. *Journal of Mammalogy* 43:262.

Gosling, N. W. 1978. Michigan's Night Gliders. *Michigan Out-of-Doors* 32(3):56, 57, 60, 61.

———. 1978. The Night Glider Nobody Notices. *Wildlife* 20:460–463.

———. 1979. Flying Squirrel. *New England Outdoors* 5(7):26–30.

———. 1980. Night Glider. *Owl* 5(2):16–21.

———. 1980. Watching the Night Gliders. *Michigan Natural Resources* 49(5):44–49.

———. 1982. Flying Squirrels. *The New York Conservationist* 36(6):34–37.

Gunderson, H. L. and J. R. Beer. 1953. The Mammals of Minnesota. *Minnesota Museum of Natural History Occasional Papers* 6:1–190.

Gupta, B. B. 1966. Notes on the Gliding Mechanism in the Flying Squirrel. *Occasional Papers, Museum of Zoology, The University of Michigan* 645:1–7.

Hall, E. R. 1981. *The Mammals of North America*. Second edition. 1:1–600. John Wiley and Sons, New York.

Hamilton, W. J., Jr. 1935. Notes on Food of Red Foxes in New York and New England. *Journal of Mammalogy* 16:16–21.

———. 1936. Seasonal Food of Skunks in New York. *Journal of Mammalogy* 17:240–246.

Handley, C. O. 1953. A New Flying Squirrel from the Southern Appalachian Mountains. *Proceedings of the Biological Society of Washington* 66:191–194.

Harper, F. 1927. The Mammals of the Okefenokee Swamp Region of Georgia. *Proceedings of the Boston Society of Natural History* 38:191–396.

Harrison, G. H. 1979. *The Backyard Birdwatcher*. Simon and Schuster, New York.

Hatt, R. T. 1931. Habits of a Young Flying Squirrel *(Glaucomys volans)*. *Journal of Mammalogy* 12:233–238.

Heaney, L. R. 1984. "Climatic Influences on Life-history Tactics and Behavior of North American Tree Squirrels." *In The Biology of Ground-dwelling Squirrels.* J. O. Murie and G. R. Michener, editors. University of Nebraska Press, Lincoln.

Heidt, G. A. 1977. Utilization of Nest Boxes by the Southern Flying Squirrel, *Glaucomys volans,* in Central Arkansas. *Arkansas Academy of Science Proceedings* 31:55–57.

Heinold, L. R. 1973. Flying Squirrels—Treetop Gliders. *Science Digest* 74(3):36–38.

Heinrichs, J. 1983. The Winged Snail Darter. *Journal of Forestry* 81:212–215, 262.

Hone, B. 1937. Chebuba—the Flying Squirrel That Motored Across the Continent. *Nature Magazine* 30:296–298.

Hooper, E. T. 1952. Records of the Flying Squirrel *(Glaucomys volans)* in Mexico. *Journal of Mammalogy* 33:109, 110.

Howell, A. H. 1915. Descriptions of a New Genus and Seven New Races of Flying Squirrels. *Proceedings of the Biological Society of Washington* 28:109–114.

———. 1918. Revision of the American Flying Squirrels. *North American Fauna* 44:1–64.

Jackson, H. H. T. 1961. *Mammals of Wisconsin.* University of Wisconsin Press, Madison.

Jordan, J. S. 1948. A Midsummer Study of the Southern Flying Squirrel. *Journal of Mammalogy* 29:44–48.

———. 1956. Notes on a Population of Eastern Flying Squirrels. *Journal of Mammalogy* 37:294, 295.

Kalm, P. 1772. *Travels into North America.* T. Lowndes, London.

Keith, L. B. and E. C. Meslow. 1966. Animals Using Runways in Common with Snowshoe Hares. *Journal of Mammalogy* 47:541.

Kelker, G. 1931. The Breeding Time of the Flying Squirrel *(Glaucomys volans volans). Journal of Mammalogy* 12:166.

King, F. H. 1883. Instinct and Memory Exhibited by the Flying Squirrel in Confinement, with a Thought on the Origin of Wings in Bats. *American Naturalist* 17:36–42.

Kittredge, J., Jr. 1928. Can the Flying Squirrel Count? *Journal of Mammalogy* 9:251–252.

Klugh, A. B. 1924. The Flying Squirrel. *Nature Magazine* 3:205–207.

Kurta, A. 1979. Southern Flying Squirrel Caught in Mist Net. *The Jack-Pine Warbler* 57:170.

Landwer, M. F. 1935. An Outside Nest of a Flying Squirrel. *Journal of Mammalogy* 16:67.

Layne, J. N. 1958. Notes on Mammals of Southern Illinois. *American Midland Naturalist* 60:219-254.

Linnaeus, C. 1758. *Systema Naturae.* Stockholm, Laurentii Salvii. 1:1–824.

Linzey, D. W. and A. V. Linzey. 1979. Growth and Development of the Southern Flying Squirrel *(Glaucomys volans volans). Journal of Mammalogy* 60:615–620.

Lowery, G. H., Jr. 1974. *The Mammals of Louisiana and Its Adjacent Waters.* Louisiana State University Press, Baton Rouge.

Luttich, S., D. H. Rusch, E. C. Meslow, and L. B. Keith. 1970. Ecology of Red-Tailed Hawk Predation in Alberta. *Ecology* 51:190–203.

MacClintock, Dorcas. 1963. Gliders of the Night. *Pacific Discovery* 16:(1):11–15.

———. 1970. *Squirrels of North America.* Van-Nostrand Reinhold Co., New York.

Madden, J. R. 1974. Female Territoriality in a Suffolk County, Long Island, Population of *Glaucomys volans. Journal of Mammalogy* 55:647–652.

———. 1976. The Behavioral Ecology of the Southern Flying Squirrel, *Glaucomys volans,* on Long Island, New York. Ph.D. dissertation, City University of New York.

Manville, R. H. 1949. A Study of Small Mammal Populations in Northern Michigan. *Miscellaneous Publications, Museum of Zoology,* The University of Michigan 73:1–83.

Maser, C., R. Anderson, and E. L. Bull. 1981. Aggregations and Sex Segregation in Northern Flying Squirrels in Northeastern Oregon, an Observation. *Murrelet* 62:54–55.

Maser, C., J. M. Trappe, and R. A. Nussbaum. 1978. Fungal-small Mammal Interrelationships with Emphasis on Oregon Coniferous Forests. *Ecology* 59:799–809.

Maslowski, K. H. 1939. The Story of Woolly, a Flying Squirrel. *Nature Magazine* 32:441–444.

McAtee, W. L. 1950. The Squirrel that Flies and Buzzes. *Nature Magazine* 43:152.

McCabe, R. A. 1947. Homing of Flying Squirrels. *Journal of Mammalogy* 28:404.

McIntyre, R. N. 1950. The "Panda Bear" of the Squirrel World. *Yosemite Nature Notes* 29(4):36–41.

McKeever, S. 1960. Food of the Northern Flying Squirrel in Northeastern California. *Journal of Mammalogy* 41:270, 271.

Mearns, E. A. 1898. A Study of the Vertebrate Fauna of the Hudson Highlands, with Observations on the Mollusca, Crustacea, Lepidoptera, and the Flora of the Region. *Bulletin of the American Museum of Natural History* 10:303–352.

Merriam, C. H. 1886. *The Mammals of the Adirondack Region.* Henry Holt and Co., New York.

Moore, C. B. 1954. *The Book of Wild Pets.* Charles T. Branford Co., Boston.

Moore, J. C. 1946. Mammals from Welaka, Putnam County, Florida. *Journal of Mammalogy* 27:49–59.

⸻ . 1947. Nests of the Florida Flying Squirrel. *American Midland Naturalist* 38:248–253.

Morton, T. 1637. *New English Canaan or New Canaan.* J. F. Stam. Amsterdam.

Mowrey, R. A., G. A. Laursen, and T. A. Moore. 1981. Hypogeous Fungi and Small Mammal Mycophagy in Alaska Taiga. *Proceedings Alaska Science Conference* 32:120–121.

Murie, O. J. 1954. *A Field Guide to Animal Tracks.* Houghton Mifflin Co., Boston.

Musser, G. G. 1961. A New Subspecies of Flying Squirrel *(Glaucomys sabrinus)* from Southwestern Utah. *Proceedings of the Biological Society of Washington* 74:119–126.

Muul, I. 1965. Day Length and Food Caches: Photoperiods Cue the Flying Squirrel. *Natural History* 74:22–27.

⸻ . 1968. Behavioral and Physiological Influences on the Distribution of the Flying Squirrel, *Glaucomys volans. Miscellaneous Publications, Museum of Zoology,* The University of Michigan 134:1–66.

⸻ . 1969. Mating Behavior, Gestation Period, and Development of *Glaucomys sabrinus. Journal of Mammalogy* 50:121.

⸻ . 1969. Photoperiod and Reproduction in Flying Squirrels, *Glaucomys volans. Journal of Mammalogy* 50:542–549.

⸻ . 1970. Intra- and Inter-familial Behavior of *Glaucomys volans* (Rodentia) Following Parturition. *Animal Behavior* 18:20–25.

⸻ . 1974. Geographic Variation in the Nesting Habits of *Glaucomys volans. Journal of Mammalogy* 55:840–844.

⸻ and J. W. Alley. 1963. Night Gliders of the Woodlands. *Natural History* 72(5):18–25.

Nelson, E. W. 1918. The Flying Squirrel *(Glaucomys volans)* and Its Relatives. *National Geographic* 32:466–468.

Osgood, F. L. 1935. Apparent Segregation of Sexes in Flying Squirrels. *Journal of Mammalogy* 16:231.

Osgood, W. H. 1900. Results of a Biological Reconnaissance of the Yukon River Region. *North American Fauna* 19:1–100.

Pearson, P. G. 1954. Mammals of Gulf Hammock, Levy County, Florida. *American Midland Naturalist* 51:468–480.

Rand, A. L. and P. Host. 1942. Results of the Archbold Expeditions, No. 45: Mammal Notes from Highland County, Florida. *Bulletin of the American Museum of Natural History* 80:1–21.

Ray, J. 1693. *Synopsis Methodica Animalium Quadrupedum et Serpentini Generis.* S. Smith and B. Walford Society, London.

Riter, R. A. and H. H. Vallowe. 1978. Early Behavioral Ontogeny in the Southern Flying Squirrel, *Glaucomys volans volans. Proceedings of the Pennsylvania Academy of Science* 52:169–175.

Rust, H. J. 1946. Mammals of Northern Idaho. *Journal of Mammalogy* 27:308–327.

Seton, E. T. 1929. *Lives of Game Animals* Vol. 4. Garden City, New York.

Shaw, G. 1801. *General Zoology.* Vol. 2. G. Kearsley, London.

Sheldon, W. G. 1971. Alopecia of Captive Flying Squirrels. *Journal of Wildlife Disease* 7:111–114.

———, W. C. Banks, and C. A. Gleiser. 1971. Osteomalacia in Captive Flying Squirrels, *Glaucomys volans. Laboratory Animal Science* 21:229–233.

Shook, R. A. 1976. Maternal Retrieving and Reproduction in the Southern Flying Squirrel, *Glaucomys volans.* M.A. thesis, Cornell University.

Smith, J. 1624. The General Historie of Virginia, New-England, and the Summer Isles. I. D. and I. H. for Michael Sparkes, London.

Snyder, L. L. 1921. An Outside Nest of a Flying Squirrel. *Journal of Mammalogy* 2:171.

Sollberger, D. E. 1940. Notes on the Life History of the Small Eastern Flying Squirrel. *Journal of Mammalogy* 21:282–293.

———. 1943. Notes on the Breeding Habits of the Eastern Flying Squirrel *(Glaucomys volans volans). Journal of Mammalogy* 24:163–173.

Sonenshine, D. E., D. G. Cerretani, G. Enlow, and B. L. Elisberg. 1973. Improved Methods for Capturing Wild Flying Squirrels. *Journal of Wildlife Management* 37:588–590.

———, D. M. Lauer, T. C. Walker, B. L. Elisberg. 1979. The Ecology of *Glaucomys volans* (Linnaeus, 1758) in Virginia. *Acta Theriologica* 24:363–377.

———, and G. E. Levy. 1981. Vegetative Associations Affecting *Glaucomys volans* in Central Virginia. *Acta Theriologica* 26:359–371.

Soper, J. D. 1970. The Mammals of Jasper National Park, Alberta. *Canadian Wildlife Service Report Series* 10:1–80.

Stack, J. W. 1925. Courage Shown by a Flying Squirrel, *Glaucomys volans. Journal of Mammalogy* 6:128, 129.

Stickel, D. W. 1963. Interspecific Relations Among Red-bellied and Hairy Woodpeckers and a Flying Squirrel. *The Wilson Bulletin* 75:203, 204.

Stoddard, H. L. 1920. The Flying Squirrel as a Bird Killer. *Journal of Mammalogy* 1:95, 96.

Svihla, R. D. 1930. A Family of Flying Squirrels. *Journal of Mammalogy* 11:211–213.

Tanner, V. M. 1927. Some of the Smaller Mammals of Mount Timpanogos, Utah. *Journal of Mammalogy* 8:250, 251.

Terres, J., editor. 1958. *The Audubon Book of True Nature Stories.* Crowell, New York.

Thomas, O. 1908. The Genera and Subgenera of the *Sciuropterus* group, with Descriptions of Three New Species. *Annals Magazine of Natural History*, series 8, 1:1–8.

Thorington, R. W. and L. R. Heaney. 1981. Body Proportions and Gliding Adaptations of Flying Squirrels (Petauristinae). *Journal of Mammalogy* 62:101–114.

Toner, G. C. 1956. House Cat Predation on Small Mammals. *Journal of Mammalogy* 37:119.

Trappe, J. M. and C. Maser. 1976. Germination of Spores of *Glomus macrocarpus* (Endogonaceae) after Passage Through a Rodent Digestive Tract. *Mycologia* 68:433–436.

Trivers, R. L. 1974. Parent-offspring Conflict. *American Zoologist* 14:249–264.

Uhlig, H. G. 1956. Reproduction in the Eastern Flying Squirrel in West Virginia. *Journal of Mammalogy* 37:295.

Walker, E. P. 1947. "Flying" Squirrels, Nature's Gliders. *National Geographic* 91:662–674.

_____. 1951. Glimpses of Flying Squirrels. *Nature* 44:81–84.

Weigl, P. D. 1969. The Distribution of the Flying Squirrels, *Glaucomys volans* and *G. sabrinus*: An Evaluation of the Competitive Exclusion Idea. Ph.D. dissertation, Duke University.

_____. 1977. "Status of the Northern Flying Squirrel, *Glaucomys sabrinus coloratus*, in North Carolina," In *Endangered and threatened plants and animals of North Carolina*, J. E. Cooper, S. S. Robinson, and J. B. Funderburg, editors, 398–400. North Carolina State Museum of Natural History, Raleigh.

_____. 1978. Resource Overlap, Interspecific Interactions and the Distribution of the Flying Squirrels, *Glaucomys volans* and *G. sabrinus*. *American Midland Naturalist* 100:83–96.

_____. and D. W. Osgood. 1974. Study of the Northern Flying Squirrel, *Glaucomys sabrinus*, by Temperature Telemetry. *American Midland Naturalist* 92:482–486.

Wells-Gosling, N. 1982. Distribution of Flying Squirrels *(Glaucomys)* in Michigan. *Michigan Academician* 14:209–216.

_____. and L. R. Heaney. 1984. *Glaucomys sabrinus*. Mammalian Species 247. *American Society of Mammalogists*.

Wrigley, R. E. 1975. Poplar Bud in the Subcutaneous Tissue of a Northern Flying Squirrel. *Canadian Field-Naturalist* 89:466.

126

Index